D0880256

JOURNEY IN
PRAYER

SEVEN DAYS OF
PRAYER WITH JESUS

John. F. Smed
with Justine Hwang
and Leah Yin

Published by Prayer Current

Published by Prayer Current
106 – 1033 Haro Street
Vancouver, BC V6E 1C8
CANADA

Abridged Text: Nathan VanderKlippe

Study Questions & Prayers: Justine Hwang

Cover Design, Illustrations & Book Layout: Leah Yin Studio

Map Grid: Erick Villagomez

www.journeyinprayer.com

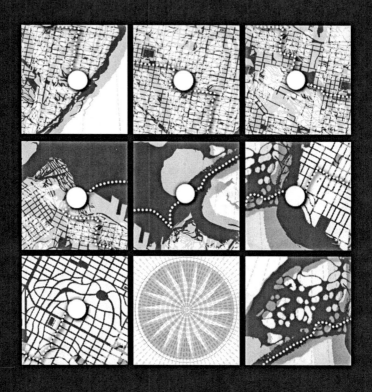

INTRODUCTION

Prayer is not everything,
but everything is by prayer.
Ray Ortlund

I am directionless. More than anything this describes my life before prayer. The year is 1970. I am seventeen. I have friends, but I feel disconnected. I graduate from high school and have a job. Still I have no sense of purpose. I do not know what to do next.

One day, in a little monastery garden, I fall on my knees and say a simple prayer, "I'm broken. Fix me, and I am yours." That very instant God reaches deep within me. God dissolves my doubt. My straying soul finds a home. One sentence – and my wandering life becomes a journey in prayer – it becomes an adventure.

Over the following weeks I keep praying but something is missing. I soon grow tired of short prayers for myself and my small world. There are rivers of feelings and thoughts within just waiting to come out. I do not know how. I do not have the words. I want to learn how to navigate life by prayer. It is pretty clear I need a guide and roadmap for this journey.

A few months after my first prayer, I head to Europe. I ski-bum and hitchhike my way around. I am reading from an old Bible I found in my parents' home. I am still saying some short prayers. I happen on to a Christian commune in the Swiss Alps. It is called L'abri, which means "shelter." This happens to be a community devoted to daily prayer. (I have long since discovered that my 'happenings' are God's plan.) L'abri is where I learn to converse with God. I learn to meditate on God's goodness and power.

It is here, high in the Alps, that I also meet my prayer guide. One night I am lying on my bed meditating on God and life. All of a sudden everything makes sense. Jesus is at the heart of God. Jesus is the one God has sent to reveal Himself to this lost and wandering teenager. I call out with the joy of discovery. I feel a pure and penetrating light enter my being. My prayer journey has become a guided adventure. Jesus is my friend and companion. He is my guide as I learn to navigate life through prayer.

Not long after I "happen upon" Jesus prayer. It is called the "Lord's Prayer." In this prayer are seven requests. In this prayer is the secret to discovering God. To pray these seven requests is to journey deeper into the life of God and deeper into life in the world.

I believe Jesus gives us this prayer to guide us in our prayer journey. He supplies a roadmap in a world with no direction of its own. He calls us to journey in prayer. He teaches us how to navigate life through prayer.

This book is a brief guide to each of the seven steps. I invite you to join me in this Journey in Prayer. If you do, I pray that your life, like mine, will never be the same.

John Smed

Our Father
in heaven,

Holy *is your name*
Your **kingdom come**
Your **will be done** *on earth*
as it is in heaven

Give us this day
our **daily bread**
Forgive us *our debts*
as we **forgive our debtors**

Lead us
not into temptation
but **deliver us** *from evil.*

Prayerful Pondering

I How do you view prayer?

2 What are the reasons you desire to pray?

3 What has been your experience(s) with prayer, if any? What has been your experience with the Lord's prayer, if any?

4 What are you hoping for your prayer journey as you delve into this book?

Feel free to use the pages of this book as a travel log of sorts. Highlight what resonates with you, challenges you, or raises questions for you. Write your own questions. Record key discoveries. Explore your thoughts by doodling or scribbling your prayers, meditations, emotions, epiphanies, enigmas – whatever God brings to you.

Most important, let Jesus guide you; he will walk with you and show you God the Father's heart for you, and for the world around you. Listen, receive, record, and remember what he wants to give you.

Prayer Practice

Prayer translates our thoughts (or what we think we understand) into a deeper reality in our hearts. Prayer is what will make the content here truly transformative – beyond filling our brains with more knowledge. For example, we may know in our minds that God is loving and good, but we may struggle to fully believe it in our hearts that God loves us and is good to us personally. Prayer helps translate our head knowledge into heart experience of God.

Plan to take some time at the end of each chapter to practice prayer, using thoughts ignited by "Prayerful Pondering" questions, "Prayer Prompts" and the sample "Personal Prayers" to guide your own prayers.

Try writing out your prayers as a record of your communication and growing relationship with God. By the end of this book, you may be surprised and encouraged to recognize God in new ways and see how he moves in your life as you pray his priorities.

My Personal Prayers

TO: Father God   **TODAY IS:** MM/DD/YY

PRAYER SPOT @ ☐ WORK ☐ HOME ☐ SCHOOL ☐

MY PRAYER

Dear God,
Here I am at the beginning of this journey:
☐ I'm not sure what to expect with this prayer thing
☐ I'm excited to see where this journey in prayer will lead me
☐
☐

Here I am with all my uncertainties and hopes:
☐ If you're there, speak to me in a way that I can hear
   and understand that it's you.
☐ I want to know who you are
☐ I need direction & purpose
☐ I need hope
☐
☐

Here I am, ready for this adventure in prayer with you.
Please be my guide. Teach me how to pray.

IN JESUS' NAME, AMEN

OUR FATHER IN HEAVEN

In giving us these words 'Our Father,'
God binds himself to us.
Luther

This is the nature of the encounter,
not that I am stumbling toward
the Abba Father, but that Abba Father
is coming towards me.
Stephen Verney

I

Prayer is not one-way. It is two-way. Think for a moment of the ways you picture prayer. Is it the penitent reciting the rosary? Is it monks spinning a prayer wheel? Is it the faithful bending low on prayer mats?

Though they may evoke powerful images, ritual incantations and relentless repetition are indications of "one-way" prayer. Prayer is not only about us getting through to God. Prayer is about God getting through to us so that we can discover his fatherly love for us. When we pray "Our Father" we are asking that we might come to know God better.

Our prayers fail if they are just one way. Luther said, "Few words and much meaning is Christian prayer. Many words and little meaning is pagan prayer." The prayer Jesus teaches us is two-way. In two-way communication we look for a reply when we speak, and we come to realize that God is eager to know and enjoy us. As we grow in our comprehension of who God is, we begin to have comfort, freedom and confidence in talking with him. We gain assurance that we are heard by him, and that he will answer and give us what we need.

We are adopted – chosen – by our heavenly Father

Several years ago, friends of mine named Stan and Lori Helm adopted their son Nicholas from Russia. By the time I met him, Nicholas was a beautiful little boy, full of life with curly auburn hair. It was hard to imagine the life he had left behind. The unsanitary orphanage had left him in ill health and covered in sores. He had seldom been held. I said to Stan, "Wow. Nicholas just won the adoption lottery with you and Lori."

Without a blink, Stan replied, "No, John. You're wrong. We won the lottery here. No one in the world could be happier than we are."

His words struck me. It made me think about "sonship" with God. He is our adoptive Father. Could it be that God is just as thrilled as Stan and Lori?

The name "father" gets God's attention

My children are the only ones who use "Dad" when addressing me. In fact it's the only name they use. If one of them calls me "mister" they probably won't get my attention. If I am not watching a hockey game, "Dad" gets through to me every time.

It is the same with God. We can try praying to a "Higher Power," we can meditate on the "Ground of Being," or we can study the "Inner Light." I doubt we will command God's attention with these generic phrases. We get God's full attention when we call him by his favorite name – "Father."

In the same way, when Jesus prays to God he calls Him "Father." Although there are 72 names for God in the Old Testament, and several more in the New Testament, every time Jesus addresses God, he calls him "Father."

Father, I thank you that you hear me always.

Father, I want those you have given me to be with me where I am, and to share my glory.

Father, if it be your will take this cup from me.

Father, forgive them, they know not what they do.

Gospel of John & Luke

Heavenly adoption made possible

How, then, do we gain the incredible privilege of calling God "Father"?

Simply this: When we trust in Jesus for forgiveness and eternal life, he confers upon us his own Royal Sonship status. By adoption, we become true sons and daughters of God. This means God views us the same as his only Son – along with all the benefits and access to him that Jesus has. In his letter to the Galatian Christians the apostle Paul explains this in dramatic terms:

But when the time had fully come, God sent his son, born of a woman, born under law, to redeem those under the law, that we might receive the full rights of sons. Because you are sons, God sent the Spirit of his Son into our hearts, the Spirit who calls out, "Abba, Father." So you are no longer a slave but a son; and since you are a son, God has made you also an heir.

Galatians 4:4-7

Not only should this take our breath away, it is the key to all effective prayer. In prayer we now call God "Abba" – an affectionate term a Jewish child uses to say "daddy." We are able to leave behind our orphan aloneness and rest in the eternal "Daddyness" of our God.

What this looks like when it comes to prayer

When you do this, you are able to come to God in freedom. You no longer have to plead your good works to earn your way in. Once you have trusted in Christ, you are God's child and nothing can ever take this from you. As the writer of the book of Hebrews writes,

Let us then approach the throne of grace with confidence, so that we may receive mercy and find grace to help us in our time of need.

Hebrews 4:16

When you talk to God, you no longer have to do penance and beat yourself up for your sins. You are forgiven the second you confess. God bears no grudge and remembers no sin. He allows you to leave behind the trappings of religion and put on the full joy of being his child.

I think of our grand-daughter Kaiya. When she comes into our home, she doesn't sit in a corner hiding, waiting for us to notice her. She runs up and simply demands attention. This is her privilege as our grand-daughter. She can ask for anything she wants. We might say no sometimes, but we could never be offended, no matter what she asks.

He is our Father "in heaven"

There are many weak and neglectful fathers in the world. But God, dwelling in the eternal reality of heaven, is the original perfect and changeless Father – "from whom all fatherhood derives." He will never abuse, neglect or use you. His love for you will never corrupt or diminish.

Ephesians 3:15

When I pray "Our Father" I know I experience the results of having such a perfect Father. I learn to receive and rest in the presence of God – where I belong. I know I can demand his attention. He will never be too busy. I can ask him for anything I need. He will never be offended. He is willing to listen. He is able to answer.

"Our Father" is the first request of this prayer

If it were up to us, we might want to jump right into prayers of confession – just to get rid of a bad conscience. We might start by crying out,

"Help Lord! I am drowning here. I need you now!"
But Jesus teaches us to bond with God as Father,
and if we start solidly with "Our Father," the rest of
our prayer will be transformed.

As we pray each request of Jesus' prayer, we keep in mind
that we are coming before a kind and generous Father.
We ask boldly, because we know he is not offended.
Teresa of Avila said, "You pay God a compliment when
you ask great things of him." Jesus said, like every good
father, your Father in heaven "delights to give good gifts
to his children." Confident and effective prayer begins
with "Our Father."

We start here. We can go no further until we know him
as Father. This precious truth should be carried into all
our requests.

Matthew 7:11

Conclusion

Remember Nicholas?

Stan and Lori went to Russia one last time to finish
the adoption procedure. After finishing the paperwork,
Stan stepped into the room and saw Nicholas in his
orphan environment. He was covered in scabies –
a bright red rash caused by small parasites. He had
blisters on the bottom of his feet, the palms of his
hands, and all over the inside of his mouth. He reeked.
The orphanage did not have money for diapers so he was
often left in his own excrement.

With his voice breaking, Stan tells me, "I just wanted to
hold him. I wanted to comfort and heal him. But more
than anything else, I wanted Nicholas to know just how
much Lori and I love him."

What a beautiful picture of God's adoption of us.
He sees us in the orphanage of the world. With a
breaking heart, he notices the scabies of our discontent,
the blisters of our unhappiness, and yes, the stench of
the sin we have too long remained in.

Rather than reject, despise and judge us, he embraces us.
He heals, cleans, and forgives us in his grace. He adopts
us to be his sons and daughters. And he takes us home to
live with him forever. Now we call him "Daddy."

Prayerful Pondering

DAY **1**   2   3   4   5   6   7

I

How do you picture prayer – as more of a religious ritual/routine or as a two-way relationship?

2

How might prayer be different by addressing God generically as a "higher power" in contrast to calling him specifically "Father"?

3

How do you feel about addressing and relating with God in such a personal way?

4

Have you ever accepted God's gift and invitation to be his child?

Prayer Prompts

When we pray "Our Father in heaven":

* We thank God for his Fatherhood. We thank him for choosing us and adopting us into his family. We enjoy and soak in his "Daddyness."

* We recognize that there is nothing we can do to make God love us less or love us more than he already does. Our striving ceases in his presence.

Prayer Practice

CreativeExploration

Prayer is conversation and relationship with God. We hear from God through his thoughts written and shared with us in his Word, the Bible, through thoughts or images he plants in our minds or hearts, through things we might see and hear from the relationships and world around us. Like all conversations and relationships, prayer is not always linear; it is rather organic, dynamically growing in multiple directions like a tree's branches and roots simultaneously expanding.

Use the space throughout this book for your prayers and explorations – to pause, pray, share with God, and listen.

Use words, images, color, and space to depict ideas and connections between various themes. You don't need to be an artist or have drawing skill; simply be open, have fun and see how God may use your scribblings to reveal insights you might not see otherwise.

My Personal Prayers

TO: Father God   **TODAY IS:** MM/DD/YY

PRAYER SPOT @ ☐ WORK   ☐ HOME   ☐ SCHOOL ☐

PRIORITY: PERSONAL RELATIONSHIP with God

REQUEST: Be present so that I may know you God

MY LIFE

You want me to come to you as your child, calling you Father. I'm not used to interacting with you in such a personal way. In the past,

☐ I've seen you as more distant and detached

☐ I've prayed as more of a ritual, but I haven't really experienced you in a personal, relational way

☐ I've seen you as an impersonal force

☐ I've treated you as a magic genie, only talking to you when I have problems and want your help solving them

☐

I am feeling ☐ excited.   ☐ amazed.   ☐ unsure.   ☐ afraid.

☐   ☐

☐   ☐

that you want this personal relationship with me. At the heart of this prayer journey, I want to get to know you for who you are.

☐ Help me put aside my preconceived notions of who you are

☐ Show me what is true of you & the kind of father you are

☐ I need you & don't want to walk this journey alone anymore

☐ I'm like an orphan - independent, self-protective, needing rescue

☐

Thank you for creating me and loving me completely as I am. Thank you that I don't have to plead my own goodness or good deeds to earn your love; it would never be enough anyway.

You choose me and adopt me as your own into your family. Thank you for your only son Jesus who makes it possible for me so to call you Father. I trust and rely on his perfect life and righteousness to make me acceptable as your child.

- ☐ Show me how deeply you love me in a way that my heart can understand & receive you
- ☐ Give me faith to believe where I struggle with doubt, freedom & confidence in my prayers
- ☐ Give my heart understanding of this reality that I am your beloved child, crafted in your image, created for a rich relationship with you
- ☐ I've treated you as a magic genie, only talking to you when I have problems and want your help solving them
- ☐
- ☐

Teach me how to pray personally, always starting and coming back to you as Father.

TO: Self

SUBJECT: My response to prayers about KNOWING YOU personally

MY REFLECTIONS & ACTIONS

☐ New knowledge, revelations or thoughts about God that came (and what difference that makes to my journey):

☐ Heart changes I felt happen during prayer, or that I felt God wanting me to change in the coming days:

☐ Next steps (decisions, actions, etc.):

MY GRATITUDE

Thank you God for:

Thanks for hearing my prayers. Give me eyes to see how you will answer in your time & in your way. Empower me to participate in how you answer.

IN JESUS' NAME, AMEN

HOLY IS YOUR NAME

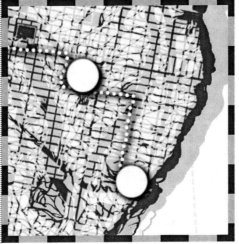

Prayer will make a man cease from sin, or sin will entice a man to cease from prayer.
John Bunyan

When we become too glib in prayer we are surely talking to ourselves.
A.W. Tozer

W hen we begin our prayer with "Our Father" we have communion with the relentless and perfect love of the Father. This love is revealed to us in Jesus, delivered to us by Jesus, and is made ours forever in Jesus. We now call God "Daddy"!

When we pray "Hallowed be your name" we are asking that God's name be held in honor and reverence. We pray to partake in his holiness and practice it in word, thought and deed.

We seldom pay as much attention to God's holiness as we do to his love. But the Old Testament highlights the holiness of God. The prophet Isaiah calls God the "Holy One of Israel" twenty-seven times! In a "meltdown" vision of God, Isaiah sees and hears heaven's greatest beings, the cherubim, continually crying out:

And they were calling to one another:
"Holy, holy, holy is the LORD Almighty;
the whole earth is full of his glory."

Isaiah 6:3

In Hebrew thought this threefold repetition is significant. God is not holy in a comparative sense, or in a superlative sense. God is holy in a super-superlative sense. While angels and men can participate in God's holiness, he is separate from all creatures in his God-holiness. God's holiness is as rich and complex as his infinite, eternal, and unchangeable being. It is revealed throughout the Bible.

1. Symbols of God's holiness

In the Old Testament there are three prominent symbols for God's holiness. These are precious jewels, blinding light, and intense fire. In one place, the prophet Ezekiel includes all three:

Above the expanse over their heads was what looked like a throne of sapphire, and high above on the throne was a figure like that of a man. I saw that from what appeared to be his waist up he looked like glowing metal, as if full of fire, and that from there down he looked like fire; and brilliant light surrounded him. Like the appearance of a rainbow in the clouds on a rainy day, so was the radiance around him. This was the appearance of the likeness of the glory of the LORD. When I saw it, I fell facedown...

Ezekiel 1:26-28

First, precious jewels indicate the purity of God. The Bible says that heaven's streets are paved with pure gold "like clear glass," its gates made of pure pearl, and its massive walls built of diamonds and jasper. This is how God describes the purity and the holiness of his kingdom.

Revelation 21:9-21

Second, the holy presence of God radiates a brilliant light – a light he has created. Anyone who sees the radiance of his glory gropes in "light blindness." Human retinas are not made for this vision.

The third symbol for God's holiness is a fierce fire that, like Moses and the burning bush, attracts and repels at the same time. In the New Testament, we are encouraged to draw near to God, but to do it "with reverence and awe, because our God is a consuming fire." His holiness is a burning passion for love, justice, righteousness, and truth. But we are warned that his fire is destructive towards anything unholy. It consumes any form of oppression, hatred, malice, envy, and greed.

Hebrews 12:29

When we put these three symbols together – precious jewels, brilliant light, and consuming fire – we are overcome by the beauty and power of God's holiness. To see God is "extreme" religion, an experience that prompts us to fall down in awe and reverence. At the same time to even get a glimpse of God's holiness is to yearn for more.

Longing for holiness

On one hand God is separate from us because, in an absolute and qualitative sense, he alone is holy in a way we can never be. On the other hand, God calls us to participate in and reflect his holiness.

"Be holy as I am holy."

Our first parents, Adam and Eve, were created in innocence and holiness. When they disobeyed God they fell from this perfect state. A world fell with them.

Imagine all humankind hurtling down a mountain road in a bus. The bus is piloted by Adam and Eve. Suddenly, the brakes fail and we slam through a concrete median and plunge down a cliff. Inside is a mangled mess. Everyone is crippled, torn, and scarred by this fall – some worse than others.

This is analogous to our spiritual nature. We are broken in the original fall of mankind.

However, no matter how broken and bruised, we are still irresistibly attracted to the glory and beauty of God's holiness. We hunger for our original fellowship with God. This is a dilemma great enough to fill a world of tragedies. We are like moths drawn to a flame.

1 Peter 1:16

We are wary of approaching the fire because our wings are flammable. At the same time, we cannot survive or be happy without its light and heat.

Though we yearn to ascend to heaven and become one with God in his holiness, we are not made for the journey. We don't have the right stuff to withstand the supernova brightness or heat of his presence.

We pray to partake in God's holiness

So how can we fulfill our longing to draw near to God's holiness without being consumed?

Isaiah asks the same question:
Who can dwell among the everlasting burnings?
His answer: *He who has clean hands and a pure heart.*

Isaiah 33:14-16

The solution to our need for holiness is Jesus. He alone has clean hands and a pure heart. He suffered an innocent death to remove our sin, as a substitute for any who will trust in him. At the moment of true belief, a believer's sin is transferred to his account.

Jesus also transfers to us his innocence. By faith in him God accepts us as holy before him. Now we dare to approach God's holy presence – with boldness!

Therefore since we have a great high priest, who has passed through the heavens, Jesus, the son of God...Let us then with confidence draw near to the throne of grace, that we may receive mercy and find grace to help in time of need.

Hebrews 4:14-16

Forgiven of sin, covered with Jesus' innocence, our wings are now made of the right stuff! We not only ascend to God's holy presence. We live there continually: "We are now seated with Christ in heavenly realms."

Ephesians 2:6

2. God's holy character is revealed in his Ten Commandments

God's holiness is revealed in the Ten Commandments, which show us what our holy Father requires of us and what he forbids.

Commands one to four are about keeping God's name holy. First, we are to worship him alone. Second, we are not to identify him with nature or anything man-made. Third, we are not to represent or misuse his name in any way. Fourth, we are to set aside one day in seven for worship, rest and good works.

Commands five to ten are about honoring God's image in the people he has made. Fifth, we are to honor our parents. Sixth to tenth, we are forbidden to kill, commit adultery, steal, falsely accuse or envy our neighbour. In a positive way we are actively to preserve and protect our neighbor's life, spouse, property, and reputation.

Because each of us is made in God's image, God's holy likeness is in every human being. Every man, woman and child, no matter how broken and bruised by sin, still bears the mark of his image and must be loved and honored for God's sake. Our concern for the name of God results in love and concern for our fellow man.

Jesus Christ reveals God's holiness

Jesus reveals the full glory and holiness of God, in his perfect person and perfect nature. Notice how John the apostle describes Jesus' holy life in the same symbols and language used of God:

We have seen his glory, the glory of the One and Only, who came from the Father, full of grace and truth...For the law was given through Moses; grace and truth came through

Jesus Christ. No one has ever seen God, but God the One and Only, who is at the Father's side, has made him known.

Therefore, it is Jesus who supremely reveals and defines holiness for the believer. Holiness is not just a matter of keeping commandments. Holiness involves following Jesus and becoming like Jesus. As we live in the presence and power of Jesus, we become, as the apostle Peter writes, "partakers in the divine nature."

The gift of Christ's holiness is like a seed sown into the human heart. In time, through prayer and the Holy Spirit, the seed sprouts, grows, and bears leaves and fruit.

Power for God's help to live holy lives

We are no more able to be holy in our own strength than we are able to escape earth's gravity. In our fallen nature we are too weak. In order to break through the force of gravity a rocket requires an upward thrust of seventeen thousand miles per hour. This requires rocket fuel. To overcome the immense gravity of our weakness and sin we need more than natural power.

We need supernatural power. This is why we ask continually to "be filled with the Holy Spirit." When we pray "Hallowed be your name" we ask for power. When we do, we will be filled with the courage and strength needed for a life of holiness. This is what happened to the early church, and it will happen again today. Consider this remarkable example from the book of Acts:

When they heard this, they raised their voices together in prayer to God... After they prayed, the place where they were meeting was shaken. And they were all filled with

John 1:4,5,14,17

2 Peter 1:4

Ephesians 5:10

the Holy Spirit and spoke the word of God boldly. All the believers were one in heart and mind. No one claimed that any of his possessions was his own, but they shared everything they had. With great power the apostles continued to testify to the resurrection of the Lord Jesus, and much grace was upon them all. There were no needy persons among them. For from time to time those who owned lands or houses sold them, brought the money from the sales and put it at the apostles' feet, and it was distributed to anyone as he had need.

This is what it means to follow Jesus. This is what holiness is all about.

Worship God's holiness

When we think of worship we might think only about a Sunday morning church service. However, there are two kinds of worship in the Bible. The first denotes a life of worship. In this sense we are to offer our words, thoughts, and deeds in a daily way to God:

Therefore, I urge you, brothers, in view of God's mercy, to offer your bodies as living sacrifices, holy and pleasing to God – this is your spiritual act of worship. Do not conform any longer to the pattern of this world, but be transformed by the renewing of your mind.

The second kind of worship is praising, proclaiming, and singing the wonders of God's person and his actions. Like the angels, we are to sing:

Holy, Holy, Holy, is the Lord God Almighty.

This is where our prayer ultimately leads and finds its fulfillment – to joyous praise of God.

Prayerful Pondering

DAY 1 **2** 3 4 5 6 7

1   Our hearts were made for worship – we all worship something. What do your prayers, thoughts, words, and actions reveal about what or who you worship?

2   Would you consider yourself to be a righteous person? How do you see yourself in light of God's holiness?

3   How do you feel about Jesus wanting to transfer his perfect holiness to you, so that God sees you as righteous? What is your response?

4   What areas of your life – thoughts, words, actions – are not honouring God's holiness? Where in your life do you want to grow in righteousness?

5   Where in the world around you do you wish for God's holiness and justice to break through? Where do you need courage to stand for righteousness and justice?

Prayer Prompts

When we pray "holy is your name":

* With reverence, we worship and honour God for his beauty and purity.

* We tremble with thanksgiving for the great price Jesus paid for our unrighteousness, so that we can be in relationship with our holy God.

* We follow Jesus, desiring to be more like him; we ask to partake in his divine nature by living in his presence and power.

* We ask for power, courage and strength needed for a life of holiness personally and in the world around us.

My Personal Prayers

TO: Father God   **TODAY IS:** MM/DD/YY

PRAYER SPOT @ ☐ WORK   ☐ HOME   ☐ SCHOOL   ☐

PRIORITY: WORSHIP of You as a HOLY God

REQUEST: Make Yourself known as you really are

MY LIFE

You are a holy God who is worth our attention and honour.
I admit it is easier for us as human beings to focus on your
love, and harder for us to concentrate on your righteousness
and justice. Maybe because looking at your perfect holiness
makes us realize how imperfect we are in light of your
righteousness. Even our best deeds and efforts at goodness
fall far short of your holiness.

Pondering your holiness, I feel:

☐ unworthy

☐ disconnected

☐ it's hard to grasp how it relates to me

☐ like my own standards of goodness are good enough for me

☐

☐

Will you show me the ways I live for my own glory/credit and build my own name and fame?

- [ ]
- [ ]
- [ ]

Your desire is for us to be transformed in our inner being, for us to be whole and holy, where we find our identity and fulfillment in deep relationship with you. Show me the areas of my life that aren't honouring to you that hinder your relationship with me:

- [ ] in my heart...

- [ ] in my thoughts...

- [ ] in my actions...

Purify our hearts, minds, actions and lives.

PRIORITY: WORSHIP of You as a HOLY God
REQUEST: Make Yourself known as you really are

MY CITY

When I look honestly at my own heart, and at the world around me, I see ways we worship ourselves above all else instead of you.

☐ I see in the corporate world greed, where profit is worshiped at the expense of people, instead of your honour

☐ I see in the entertainment world celebrity worship, seeking our own pleasure at all cost, to the detriment of others instead of worshiping you & seeking what pleases you

☐

MY RESPONSE

Though it's hard for me to grasp, you want me to participate in living out your righteousness in the world.

☐ Give me an appetite for what is holy & right in your eyes.

☐ Give me a growing uneasiness and dissatisfaction with what isn't pleasing to you.

☐ Open my eyes to see how I can stand for your righteousness.

☐ Fill me with your presence, power, courage, strength to live in a way that honours you in my own life & to be a conduit for your holiness to the city around me.

☐

MY REFLECTIONS & ACTIONS

☐ New knowledge, revelations or thoughts about God that came (and what difference that makes to my journey):

☐ Heart changes I felt happen during prayer, or that I felt God wanting me to change in the coming days:

☐ Next steps (decisions, actions, etc.):

MY GRATITUDE

Thank you God for:

Thanks for hearing my prayers. Give me eyes to see how you will answer in your time & in your way. Empower me to participate in how you answer.

IN JESUS' NAME, AMEN

Your Kingdom Come

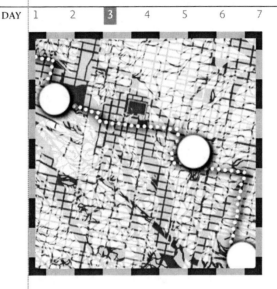

*To clasp the hands in prayer is
the beginning of an uprising against
the disorder of the world.*
Karl Barth

*So that your prayer may have its full
weight with God, see that ye be in charity
with all men... Nor can you expect to
receive any blessing from God while you
have not charity towards your neighbor.*
Richard Sibbes

The Bible's concept of kingdom is rich but not complicated. In its simplest sense, when Jesus tells us to pray "Your kingdom come," he emphasizes that we are to live our lives in light of his triumphant return which will happen at the end of the world. No present suffering, discouragement, or opposition can overcome our confident hope that Jesus will soon restore all things.

But Jesus' kingdom does not come all at once. It comes in stages.

First, Jesus is our "Forever King." As part of the Trinity, Jesus has always ruled and reigned with the Father and Holy Spirit.

Second, when Jesus lived and died for us, he became our "Redeemer King." His death is an inauguration and his resurrection is a coronation. In Paul's letter to the Philippian Christians, Paul writes:

Philippians 2:8-11

God exalted him to the highest place and has given him the name that is above every name, that at the name of Jesus every knee should bow, in heaven and on earth and under the earth, and every tongue confess that Jesus Christ is Lord.

Third, Jesus is our "Coming King," the one who will judge and recreate all things at the end of the world. He promises that he will return, vindicate his faithful followers and reveal the injustice of those who reject him:

Matthew 24:30,31

They will see the Son of Man coming on the clouds of the sky, with power and great glory. And he will send his angels with a loud trumpet call, and they will gather his elect from the four winds, from one end of the heavens to the other.

Jesus' kingdom is coming in a final sense because he is coming again to renew the entire creation and to bring in the new age.

When we pray "Your kingdom come," we pray as loyal subjects who acknowledge his eternal creator-lordship. We pray as those who accept his saving work in his incarnation. We cry out in eager expectation of his coming again to renew all things.

A modern day metaphor

Living in a western democracy, we may find it difficult to relate to the concept of living in a kingdom. But consider for a moment a modern parallel. Imagine a Fortune 500 company taking over a smaller company that has fallen on hard times.

The buyer is Dominion Realty, a national corporation with offices and operations all over Canada. Dominion buys out Independent Realty – a smaller outfit. The day after the takeover, the Dominion boss forms a transition team with these instructions, "You have three years to make Independent into a Dominion company. I do not want to chop this company up. I want to renew and rebuild it. Win over as many employees and managers as possible. And call me any time you need me."

Dominion and Independent may be in similar lines of work, but they have different cultures. Dominion is about team work. Independent values individual accomplishments above everything. At Independent, the philosophy is "pull your weight or you're dead weight." Dominion is concerned about company culture. Independent is concerned about the bottom line.

The transition team arrives on site and gets to know Independent.

After a month of careful listening, they gather everyone together to make an announcement.

Corinne, the spokesperson, starts by stating the situation in simple terms. "We are going to have a Dominion company. Nothing can stop that. But don't think for a minute we want to get rid of you! We want to win you over. Dominion is a great company with a great boss. If you are willing to get on board you can be part of a fantastic future. If not, you will probably quit before we have to let you go."

She finishes, "Bottom line, the boss is coming soon. Our only job is to get ready for his coming."

Getting ready for the return of the King

Jesus is the Dominion boss. This world, insofar as it does not acknowledge his present lordship, is "Independent." The time between his first and second coming is the three-year transition.

As Christians, we are the transition management team. This second coming is unstoppable. It is our job to arrange everything to prepare for that coming and to win people over for our coming king.

During this interim period, we not only announce Jesus coming, we teach, carry out and model the plans of our coming king. Someone said, "Christians are building show homes. Their job is to show what the new neighborhood will look like."

Let's return to our illustration.

At the outset, there are some who want nothing to do with the Dominion takeover. The Independent boss does not take long to make his views known:

"Everything we have worked so hard for is being ruined!"

Before long, he quits, sets up a competitor company and takes some Independent staff with him.

However, other Independent employees are willing to take a look at Dominion. Most lived on long hours and low wages. They were constantly concerned about job security.

The Dominion team wants to reverse this trend. Peter, who is on the transition team, comes up to Jim, an account manager for Independent.

"Jim, I notice you let Frank go last week. Why? He seemed to be working hard."

Jim answers, "Yeah, he tried. But he couldn't cut it."

Peter reflects for a minute.

"Jim, I want you to give Frank another chance. Let's get him some training if he needs it. He seems to have a good attitude. I think we can make progress."

"Okay. You're the boss."

"Actually I'm not. I just work for him – like you!

"And by the way, Jim, I notice you let six or seven others go in the past six months. I wonder if we shouldn't ask them back, too."

Eyebrows raised, Jim stares at Peter.

He asks, "I don't get it. What kind of company wants to keep everyone on payroll and even hire people back?"

Peter just smiles. He can see things from Jim's perspective.

"I understand. You see, it's our boss. He likes to rebuild things. He likes to make winners out of losers."

He continues, "When our boss was younger, he suffered a personal catastrophe. Everyone thought he was finished. No one gave him a chance.

"But somehow, he came back. It happened suddenly – you might say miraculously. That's why he always gives a second chance."

Jim listens. "Interesting. But what about you?"

"I'm glad you ask. I was a workaholic, so bad that I lost my wife and my kids. Even my business went under.

"I was a useless wreck when, out of nowhere one day, the boss called me. He asked if I wanted to do some transition work. He thought I might be good at it. Now I get to help other shipwrecks like myself. And it feels good – really worthwhile."

"Okay, that makes some sense. But what about the others on your team. What's their story?"

"Pretty much similar to mine. Corinne was forced to quit a high-paying job for a fast-food joint after leaving her abusive husband. Phil has terminal cancer. The boss offered him this job as a way to finish life on a high note. And here he is. Going out in a blaze of glory!"

Jim thought he saw tears welling up in Peter's eyes.

"You see, Jim, this is not just a job. Frankly, I love the boss. He could ask me to shovel manure and I would – in a minute!"

Jim didn't say anything.

He didn't know what to say.

Sharing our story

Taking our cue from Peter, we can understand a little more about Jesus' coming kingdom. Sharing what Jesus has done for us is not just a job. It's about loyalty to our coming king. While we wait for his return we share our story. We explain to others how Jesus has established the kingdom of God once and for all.

We explain that God owns every last atom, proton, and electron in the universe. He is the creator-king and every man, woman and child owes him worship and thanks. He is the all-powerful king of all kings.

Then I heard every creature in heaven and on earth and under the earth and on the sea, and all that is in them, singing: "To him who sits on the throne, and to the Lamb be praise and honor and glory and power, for ever and ever!"

Revelations 5:13

Some Christians feel that talking about the end of the world seems foreboding – even frightening. However, we need to remember this "ending" is a great beginning. All the history of this world is only a brief introduction, merely the cover of a book.

We haven't even gotten to the good stuff yet. In the rest of the story, sorrow, sickness, tears and death will be left behind. What is weak becomes strong. Small fragments of precious faith are refined and perfected. Best of all, anyone who wants to start fresh and to live forever in unimaginable bliss is welcome to become a part of his new world. We – redeemed, but still sinners – get to humbly pass out the invitations!

Living out the values of the kingdom

But there is more to the kingdom than sharing the story with others. We also ask for his grace and Spirit to live out the values and character of his coming kingdom today. We look for our present world to change as a result of his kingdom coming into our lives.

Remember what the boss says, "I want a Dominion company when I come back."

Dominion does not come in to end the doing of business! It comes, instead, to end the way business is done.

This is true of Jesus' transition team, too. Though we have a new king, we live in the same communities, go to the same schools, and work in the same marketplace. We know "down and outers." We know "up and outers." We know "way-outers" too.

We are tasked with bringing the joy of God's kingdom to them, today. When we pray "Your kingdom come," we daily apply our prayers to the deep needs of our cities.

An example in Vancouver

In our city of Vancouver, Lorn Epp directs More than a Roof ministry. It works with local and civic leaders to help the impoverished and mentally ill by giving them the dignity of their own place to live.

Lorn came into this line of ministry after his family had to help one of its own members who struggled with mental illness. It took everything this family had to keep this loved one off of the streets. Jesus used this time to prepare Lorn for helping others in similar circumstances. More than a Roof now serves hundreds of those struggling with mental illness or recovering from addictions. All are welcome. All are given the dignity of a home to live in.

Lorn puts it this way, "Christians need to remember the great commandment as well as the great commission. Jesus taught us to love our neighbor as well as to lead him to faith." The theme verse of Lorn's life is:

Is it not to share your food with the hungry and to provide the poor wanderer with shelter – when you see the naked, to clothe him...Your people will rebuild the ancient ruins and will raise the age old foundations; you will be called Repairer of Broken Walls, Restorer of Streets with Dwellings. *Isaiah 58:6,7,12*

The outcome of genuine faith, and a genuine desire to see God's kingdom come, will always be a life of kindness, justice and good works.

Illustrating the role of prayer in preparing for his coming kingdom

Back to our story.

Jim from accounting is almost ready to join Dominion for good. He has one more important question to ask. He walks up to Peter and asks, "Tell me. Where do you get your energy and resolve to keep going? Frankly, I want some."

Peter smiles. "Jim, each of us has a direct line to the boss. If you want you can have one too. He tells each of us to call him day or night for any reason whatever. He always answers. And he never seems in a rush. I can't remember him ever ending the conversation. When I have to say 'goodbye,' he says 'Okay, but call back soon.'"

Like Peter, God's children have a direct line, too. It is prayer. We have unlimited personal and direct access to our father for his friendship, strength and wisdom. There is no obstacle that we cannot face with him at our side. There is no challenge we cannot overcome by his grace and presence through prayer.

Postscript

At the end of three years the boss comes back. Unannounced, he enters from the back. It is pretty obvious who he is.

Everyone has been waiting for this day. As he goes through the offices he starts to smile. He has a feel for things, and things feel good. Peter, Corrine, Ted and Phil look excited and a bit nervous at the same time. Jim feels weak at the knees.

He gathers them together and, with a deep and genuine smile, says, "I like what I see. It feels like a Dominion company. I am really happy each of you is here. You are becoming a real team."

He turns to face Corrine and the other leaders. "Corrine, Peter, Ted, Phil – you have done it again! Good work. It's been a blast hasn't it?"

He turns and looks at Jim, "Oh, and you Jim. From the day I bought Independent I knew you were going to be a part of us. Welcome home."

He adds, "I want you to introduce share options for every employee. I want them to get a share of our success. This location is yours to run for me. Enjoy it. You have already proven you will do a great job."

I hope the point is clear. The greatest joy of believers will be to see the face of Jesus when he comes in his glory. There will be no mistaking him in that day. We will be eager and anxious for him to give his verdict on our work. When we pray "Your kingdom come," we pray to be ready for that day. We ask to hear,

Well done good and faithful servant. You have been faithful with a few things; I will put you in charge of many things. Come and share your master's happiness."

Matthew 25:23

Prayerful Pondering

I   By which values do you find yourself living –
Independent or Dominion? What do your prayers,
thoughts, words, and actions reveal about who or
what you are most loyal to?

2   What is attractive to you about the Dominion way
of life? What is preventing you from more fully
embracing it?

3   What is your view of the Dominion boss, Jesus?
What is your relationship with him? Will you give
your loyalty to him?

4   Jesus gives you unlimited personal and direct access
to the Father for friendship, strength and wisdom.
Where do you need his strength and wisdom to live
by Dominion values in your own life?

5   What relationships or situations in the world
around you might Jesus be asking you to represent
his Dominion values? What is one way you can do
that this week?

Prayer Prompts

When we pray "Your kingdom come":

* We give our loyalty to Jesus and acknowledge his creator lordship and leadership in our lives. We ask to be used to lead others to know Jesus too.

* We cry out in eager expectation of his coming again to renew all things. We pray for the deep needs of our city, for his values of restoration and rebuilding to reign.

* We confess our inclination to deny mercy and pass judgment and our tendency to walk by on the other side when we see someone in rags or other adversity. We cry out for a heart that truly cares for someone in need.

* We ask for the Spirit, grace, courage and wisdom to live out the values and character of Jesus' coming kingdom today. We ask for integrity of life, where deeds of justice match our words of love.

My Personal Prayers

TO: Father God   **TODAY IS:** MM/DD/YY

PRAYER SPOT @ ☐ WORK ☐ HOME ☐ SCHOOL ☐

PRIORITY: Grow to SURRENDER to you & your ways as KING

REQUEST: Let your reign be established

MY LIFE

Thank you that Jesus is coming again as King one day. I admit it's hard to pray for "your kingdom come - because if I'm honest, I really am living for myself and building my own "kingdoms."

Pondering your desire to lead my life as my boss/king, I feel:

☐ I often/always think I know best

☐ I want to maintain control of my life

☐

☐

I admit some of my struggle to let you lead my life is because I don't know or trust you that well because:

- ☐ I struggle with authority figures
- ☐ I'm too busy to think of you
- ☐ I have preconceived notions of you
- ☐
- ☐

Please show me what kind of leader and king you really are. I am ready to give you leadership because:

- ☐ I've made a mess of things
- ☐ I'm tired & my own way of doing things has exhausted me
- ☐ I feel powerless
- ☐
- ☐

Help me to increasingly trust you with complete leadership over my life, just as Jesus submitted his life to be ruled by you completely.

MY CITY

Jesus, Thank you for the work you are doing in my city.
Strengthen its foundation to be on your kingdom values. Let
your kingdom come in my city. As I pass through different
districts of my city,

☐ the business hub

☐ the artsy upscale parts of town

☐ the cultural enclaves

☐ the neighbourhood where I live

☐ the area where I work/where my office is

☐

☐

I find it hard to recognize your "dominion." It's even harder
to see you in places of inequality and suffering, like

☐ in the hidden conflicts in broken families behind closed doors

☐ or the rundown poverty-stricken parts of town that I avoid
  because it's too uncomfortable to see, or it's too inconvenient
  or large of a problem to help

☐

☐

REQUEST: Let your reign be established

MY CITY

In seeing the challenges of my city, if I'm honest,
I struggle with:

☐ pride, I am beyond helping

☐ fear of involvement

☐ doubt of making any lasting difference

☐

☐

From the scale of my heart to the city's core, show me
the needs and dysfunctions that your power can restore.
Your light and power is always stronger than the darkness
and challenges. Shine & break through to restore & renew
the city and the people - because of how you love them.

MY RESPONSE

Give me a heart that cares to move in integrity with your
kingdom values, and wisdom and courage to participate in
your restoring work. Help me not to turn a blind eye to
the emptiness, brokenness or darkness, but teach me to pray
for your restoration to come. Preserve in me a hopeful and
tender heart, not calloused by cynicism or apathy. Show me
how my life, prayers, and actions are connected to "your
kingdom coming" more fully in the world around me. Lead
me and empower me to live as you want me to.

TO: Self

SUBJECT: My response to prayers about YOUR KINGDOM & leadership

MY REFLECTIONS & ACTIONS

☐ New knowledge, revelations or thoughts about God that came (and what difference that makes to my journey):

☐ Heart changes I felt happen during prayer, or that I felt God wanting me to change in the coming days:

☐ Next steps (decisions, actions, etc.):

MY GRATITUDE

Thank you God for:

Thanks for hearing my prayers. Give me eyes to see how you will answer in your time & in your way. Empower me to participate in how you answer.

IN JESUS' NAME, AMEN

YOUR WILL BE DONE
ON EARTH AS IT IS IN HEAVEN

DAY 1   2   3   **4**   5   6   7

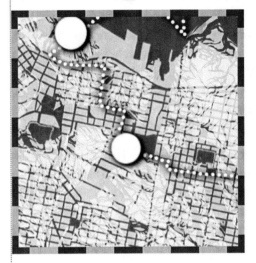

The purpose of prayer is not to get man's will done in heaven, but to get God's will done on earth.
Warren Wiersbe

Prayer transforms our vision and makes us see it in the light of God
Thomas Merton

The purpose of all prayer is to find God's will and to make that will our prayer.
Catherine Marshall

God's will is rich, deep and multifaceted. In its most comprehensive sense, God's will is the environment within which all creatures exist. When Jesus asserts that God's will is "done in heaven," he means that God's will is the symphony to which all heaven and its myriad angelic hosts are tuned. This music is so vast and deep and rich that all the songs of heaven are a part of it. God creates the world, "while the morning stars sang together and all the angels shout for joy." Think of the world's great symphonies – *The Planets, The Pastoral Symphony, The Four Seasons.* Throw in Purcell's *Trumpet Voluntary* and imagine all rolled into one harmonious, beautiful and joyous song.

Job 38:7

We are to do God's will on earth 'as in heaven' because God's angels in heaven are in perfect harmony with God's will. Thousands and thousands of angels are in "joyful assembly" because they are tuned to God's will. The cherubim – awesome angelic beings who surround God's throne – are so tuned to God's will that their very movements are in synch with God, "Wherever the Spirit would go they will go."

Hebrews 12:22
Ezekiel 1:20

If we are to carry out God's will on earth as in heaven, it is more than a matter of simple obedience. We need to share the angels' inner harmony with the will of God. Our wills need to be tuned to God's will. This is the transformational goal of this command. The apostle Paul points us in this direction:

Romans 12:2-3

Do not conform any longer to the pattern of this world, but be transformed by the renewing of your mind. Then you will be able to test and approve what God's will is – his good pleasing and perfect will.

54

Yet the reality is that his will is not done "on earth."
From earliest history, there is a dissonance on earth because
we have edited God from the songs of our lives. This
dissonance manifests itself as exploitation, propaganda,
violence, cruelty, and all other forms of injustice. It has
spread through all places through all history.

Yet God does not surrender his song to this discord.
He renews the concert of his will –his perfect plan and
purpose – to centre stage in history. When Jesus comes
to the stable in Bethlehem, on earth we hear heaven's
music once again:

*Suddenly a great company of the heavenly host appeared
with the angel, praising God and saying, "Glory to God in the
highest & on earth peace to men on whom his favor rests."* Luke 2:13

When Jesus surrenders his life on a Roman cross,
we imagine a song of lament – funeral eulogy –
as the earth itself groans and the skies mourn in
darkness. This song is so heart-rending and sorrowful
that to hear it is to remember it forever.

When Jesus rises from the dead, we spring from
the minor key. We hear the pizzicato of the strings,
the dance of the woodwinds and uproarious thunder of
the percussion. Our hearts leap and creation dances to the
triumphant chorus. This song spreads in overwhelming
joy and healing, "as far as the curse is found."

*Sing to the LORD a new song;
sing to the LORD, all the earth.*

*Sing to the LORD, praise his name;
proclaim his salvation day after day.* Psalm 96:1,2,11,13

Psalm 96:1,2,11,13

Let the heavens rejoice, let the earth be glad;
let the sea resound, and all that is in it,

Let the fields be jubilant, and everything in them.
Then all the trees of the forest will sing for joy;

They will sing before the LORD,
for he comes, he comes to judge the earth.
He will judge the world in righteousness and
the peoples in his truth.

When we pray "Your will be done on earth as it is in heaven," we are asking to once again hear the symphony of God's will. We want to tune our lives to this music and to become a joyous part of its song. We want to obey God, but we want to do it with a song of joy and thanks in our heart.

The scope of this prayer

When we ask that "your will be done on earth as it is in heaven," we pray for at least three things. First, we ask to accept God's will. Second, we pray to approve God's will Third, we pray to do God's will.

First we pray to accept God's will

God's will is done – always and everywhere.
To try to live outside God's will is impossible. His will permeates all existence. In one sense, to oppose God's will is futile. We cannot break God's will – in the sense of preventing him from doing what he decides to do. We can only be broken in the attempt.

An ancient pagan king of Babylon, Nebuchadnezzar, found out about God's unbreakable will the hard way.

One day he decides to take credit for his kingdom glory.
As he walks the palace walls and surveys Babylon and all
its splendors – perhaps looking at the hanging gardens,
he boasts;

*Is not this the great Babylon I have built as the royal
residence, by my mighty power and for the glory of
my majesty?*

Daniel 4:30

For this pride, Nebuchadnezzar was stripped of his
throne and made to crawl on all fours until his hair
looked like eagle's feathers and his claws like bird's claws.
When he finally wakes up to his folly, the first thing he
proclaims throughout his kingdom is nothing and no
one stop God from doing what he chooses to do:

*His dominion is an eternal dominion; his kingdom endures
from generation to generation. All the peoples of the earth
are regarded as nothing. He does as he pleases with the
powers of heaven and the peoples of the earth. No one can
hold back his hand or say to him: "What have you done?"*

Daniel 4:33-35

Therefore, when we pray "Your will be done" we affirm
that God's rule and reign extends everywhere. We accept
the limitation of our freedom when we pray "your will
be done." Only God is absolutely free and undetermined.

Our God is in heaven; he does whatever pleases him.

Psalm 115:3

Everything in heaven and earth is created. God alone is
creator. Every creature is dependent on the creation.
He stands above the creation in his self-determination
and freedom. Our freedom is limited by our nature,
our environment, and by God's plan and purposes.

Therefore, when we pray "Your will be done" we worship God and ensure that all of our plans and purposes begin and end with "Deo Volenti" – "God willing."

Second, we ask to approve God's will

When we accept God's will we do not just resign ourselves to it. God's will is not fate. His will is a living expression of his being and reveals his wisdom, justice, and truth. Once we get to know God's will and to accept it, we soon learn to approve it:

Do not conform any longer to the pattern of this world,
but be transformed by the renewing of your mind.
Then you will be able to test and approve what
God's will is – his good, pleasing and perfect will.

Romans 12:2-3

Approving God's will is not always easy. Consider how the biblical character Job interprets God's will. Catastrophe strikes Job from all sides. He loses his property to looters, his animals to fire, and his children to a freak storm. What Job says reveals that he accepts and approves God's will:

At this, Job got up and tore his robe and shaved his head.
Then he fell to the ground in worship and said:
"Naked I came from my mother's womb, and naked
I will depart. The LORD gave and the LORD has taken
away; may the name of the LORD be praised." In all this,
Job did not sin by charging God with wrongdoing.

Job 1:20-22

This is not resignation. Job does not believe in fate. He knows that God's will is over every event of his life. He knows that God is not capricious or malicious, in spite of how circumstances appear. He believes that God has a higher purpose, even if Job cannot discern it.

Nor does Job believe he is being punished for his sins.
He lives by grace and not by karma. When his "friends"
insist that he is getting what he deserves, Job maintains
that God is not judging him as an offender, but is testing
him as his child. To that end he refuses to characterize
God as a heartless judge. This is the main theme of Job.
He knows that Satan's tempting is God's testing.

This is important. When we pray, "Your will be done"
we are asking to understand and approve God's will –
especially in the hard times.

The best example of accepting and approving of God's
will is Jesus Christ himself. In his final days on earth,
Jesus is in the garden of Gethsemane. He knows what
agony is in store for him at the cross. He knows that he
will be cruelly murdered. He already feels the burden of
mankind's sin. In this terrible moment, Jesus does not
just wrestle with fate. In prayer, he struggles with,
and within, the will of God:

*Then he said to them, "My soul is overwhelmed with sorrow
to the point of death. Stay here and keep watch with me."
Going a little farther, he fell with his face to the ground and
prayed, "My Father, if it is possible, may this cup be taken
from me. Yet not as I will, but as you will."*

Matthew 26:38-39

Jesus' sorrow is real, and his pain is intense, yet he
realizes that his heavenly father permits his suffering for
the highest of purposes – the salvation of a universe!

In the same way, the key to our growth in grace is to pray
to approve of God's will for our lives:
I cry out to God, who fulfills his purpose for me.

Psalm 57:2

In believing prayer, we learn to connect our present troubles to the good and perfect will of God. We refuse to believe that chance rules our lives. We withstand the temptation to imagine that God is capricious or malicious. We know he has a higher purpose and that he is not dealing with us as our sins deserve. Listen to what Peter the apostle says about God's higher purposes:

I Peter 4:12-19

Dear friends, do not be surprised at the painful trial you are suffering, as though something strange were happening to you. But rejoice that you participate in the sufferings of Christ, so that you may be overjoyed when his glory is revealed. If you are insulted because of the name of Christ, you are blessed, for the Spirit of glory and of God rests on you. So then, those who suffer according to God's will should commit themselves to their faithful Creator and continue to do good.

As we bring our troubles to Jesus in prayer – asking his will to be done – we approve the will of our Father in heaven. We see our sufferings in the greater reality of his good, acceptable, and perfect will. In prayer we "turn crisis to Christ." Our heart becomes tuned to his heart and we sing the song of grace.

This is good news when it comes to prayer! Once we learn to accept and approve of God's will, we are able to pray with great effect and assurance. When we ask according to God's will, our will is tuned and in harmony with his will. We not only know God's will from the Bible, we have learned to approve his will from our spiritual growth and experience. Jesus calls this harmony with God's will "abiding."

I am the vine; you are the branches...If you abide in me and my words remain in you, ask whatever you wish, and it will be given you. This is to my Father's glory, that you bear much fruit, showing yourselves to be my disciples.

John 15:5,7,8

Those who abide in Jesus learn to pray according to God's will, and have an inner assurance that their prayers are answered.

Third, we pray to do God's will on earth as in heaven

God's will is perfect. His will is unchangeable but is living and alive as God is. In order to make his will clear, God has given us commands as a rule and guide for life. He requires our obedience to his laws.

Once again, heaven is our example. The chief joy of the angels is to obey God's commands. In fact, we have no biblical examples of angels acting independently of Gods' commands:

The Lord has established his throne in heaven, and his Kingdom rules over all.

Praise the Lord, you his angels, you mighty ones who do his bidding and obey his word. Praise the Lord, all his heavenly hosts, you his servants who do his will.

Psalm 103:19-21

For us to pray and do God's will 'as in heaven' we are not to obey God grudgingly, but to rejoice in obeying God.

God's commands are more than rules. Rules are simply legal boundaries. They are impersonal. Consider sporting events. The referee who executes the rules does not have to feel passionate about them. God's commands, in contrast, are not just rules.

They express his holy character. They express his identity. God is not a disinterested referee who just makes sure the game is kept "in hand." He is passionate about his laws – for them to be kept – from the heart.

God's will includes a passion for justice. His will includes grief and sorrow for victims of injustice. To do God's will in its fullest sense, is more than mere obedience. True obedience includes sharing his passion for justice and his compassion for victims of injustice. God is internally committed to justice. In fact, justice is an attribute of God. His laws are supremely just. He appoints those who have authority in family, society and church to maintain justice and stop oppression.

Cruelty and injustice happen every day in every city. Women and children are molested. Many are physically abused – in their own homes. Innocent parties are left in ruins after ugly divorce battles. New immigrants are subject to prejudice and given demeaning work. The mentally ill are sent out of crowded hospitals and left to fend for themselves on the streets. From their deepest heart, each victim cries questions of anguish: "Is my suffering God's will? Does God care? Is there justice? Will God rescue me from my oppressor?"

When we ask to do God's will, we commit to listen to these kinds of questions. We ask to know and to share God's passion for justice and his grief at injustice. We pray to hear the cries of the victim and ask to be willing to be the answer. Our prayer for God's will, therefore, is effective only if we share God's love of justice and hatred of oppression exploitation and violence.

Deeds are an outcome of prayer

It is not enough to just know God's will, or to pray for God's will to be done, we need grace and courage to obey and carry it out. The rubber has to hit the road. This is the "earth" where Jesus' will is to be done.

When we pray, "Your will be done on earth as it is in heaven," we are committing to doing God's will. Facing the enormous social problems in our cities today, we do not say, "What has this got to do with me? This is the government's job." We cannot say, "This is not my problem. This is part of the wickedness of the world. I am separate from that. I have to protect and preserve my righteousness." Instead we pray, "Your will be done in me and through me." We pray for wisdom and courage to get involved with our city. God gives us wisdom. He will raise up leaders and servants to do his will.

In a *Showers for the Shelterless* program, we partner with others in our community to serve the homeless and mentally ill. We provide a gourmet coffee, breakfast and newspaper for our homeless guests. We visit and get to know them. We provide a "valet service" for their carts and dogs. The homeless won't come in if their belongings are unattended.

At a local housing project, we have worked with *More Than a Roof* to bring the gospel and community development to the tenants who live there. With *Genesis Vancouver,* a ministry to sexually exploited women and their children we pray for and seek to serve the sexually exploited – to deliver them not only from pimps and "Johns" but also from a culture that exploits us all.

We partner and pray for Genesis Vancouver to provide safe houses and day programs for the sexually exploited and their children.

There is a connection between our praying for justice and justice coming to pass. Speaking to Israel while exiled in Babylon, Jeremiah reminds his people to seek justice for their city.

Seek the peace and prosperity of the city to which I carried you in exile. Pray to the Lord for it, because if it prospers, you too will prosper...For I know the plans I have for you, declares the Lord, plans to prosper you and not to harm you, plans to give you hope and a future. Then you will call upon me and I will listen to you.

Jeremiah 29:7,11,12

Notice how prayer for the city is commanded. Notice how God promises he will answer with urban peace and prosperity.

Another striking passage is found in Isaiah 58. As in Jeremiah, there is a connection between our prayers for urban renewal and God's promise to hear this prayer. However, something crucial is added. God's answer to our prayer is that he sends us into the city to be his agents of transformation. He will rebuild the city. He will do it through those who pray. We become the answer to our own prayer!

*Is this not the kind of fasting that I have chosen: to loose the
chains of injustice and untie the cords of the yoke, to set the
oppressed free and break every yoke? Is it not to share your
food with the hungry and to provide the poor wanderer
with shelter ...Then your light will break forth like the
dawn and your healing will quickly appear; then your
righteousness will go before you and the glory of the Lord
will be your rear guard. Then you will call and the Lord will
answer; you will cry for help and he will say Here am I...
Your people will rebuild the ancient ruins and will raise
up the age old foundations; you will be called Repairer of
Broken Walls, Restorer of Streets with Dwellings.*

Isaiah 58:6-12

The implication is clear. As God's people we are to pray
for his will to be done on earth. We are to become deeply
engaged with the needs of our city. God will answer
our prayer as we do so. He will rescue the needy and
establish safe neighborhoods. The way God renews the
city is by sending his people to carry out this mandate.
This is how his will is done on earth as it is in heaven.

Let it sink in. Let it take your breath away. As we seek
God's will in prayer, and then carry it out, we will
embody the transformation the oppressed cry out for!
We will see substantial healing and restoration at the
heart of our city.

What a marvelous encouragement to prayer.

Prayerful Pondering

1   God desires for us to want his will. How open is
    your heart to tuning in and hearing the symphony
    of God's will for your life? What is hindering you
    from wanting God's will?

2   Where are you struggling to know and accept God's
    will in your life currently? Where do you need Jesus
    to settle your heart to his will? How does it make
    you feel knowing Jesus also struggled and suffered
    with and within the will of God?

3   When you look at the world around you, where do
    you feel and see the dissonance of injustice?

4   Where might God be asking you to pray for and
    engage with the needs around you, to be involved
    in his will to renew and restore the city and its
    people? How willing are you to be the answer to
    your prayers?

5   Who is your neighbour, practically speaking?
    How is God asking you to love them?

Try praying through the newspaper one day. Ask God to show you his perspective and heart for the people, places and problems that are in your city and world. Pray for his will to be done.

Prayer Prompts

DAY   1   2   3   **4**   5   6   7

When we pray "Your will be done on earth as it is in heaven":

*   We surrender and ask for our will to be in harmony with, and to do God's will.

*   We bring our joys and troubles to Jesus in prayer, asking him to settle our hearts to his will. We ask to see our sufferings in the greater reality of his good and perfect will.

*   We pray to hear the cry of the victim. We pray for passion for justice, for compassion and rehabilitation of both the victims and offenders of injustice.

*   We ask to be willing to be the answer, to have wisdom and courage to obey and carry out his will on earth, and to get involved in the needs of our city.

My Personal Prayers

DAY 1   2   3   **4**   5   6   7

TO: Father God   **TODAY IS:** MM/DD/YY

PRAYER SPOT @ ☐ WORK   ☐ HOME   ☐ SCHOOL   ☐

PRIORITY: Knowing & extending your will

REQUEST: Fulfill YOUR WILL & good pleasure

MY LIFE

Your will is rich, deep, and multifaceted. Your Word to us through the Bible tells us that your will is good, perfect, and pleasing. Yet I honestly struggle with praying for "your will to be done" because:

☐ my own will can be so strong

☐ I think my will is best

☐ I struggle to understand or know what your will is

☐ I don't trust your will to be good

☐

☐

Show me more of who you really are so I can grow in trusting your will.

I ask for your will to be done specifically in the area of:

☐ my career

☐ my relationships

☐ a specific decision

☐

☐

Help me to discern what your will is & give me a willingness to trust and follow you in your will & ways.

I also bring to you my present difficulties that are causing me:

☐ worry.   ☐ grief.   ☐ struggle.   ☐ pain & suffering.

☐

I'm struggling with: ☐ doubts. ☐ questions. ☐ tiredness. ☐ despair.

☐

Settle my heart to trust you and to know your presence amidst the challenges. Help me to give all of myself and my will to you, because you gave all of yourself for us when you gave up your son Jesus. Thank you Jesus that you know our struggles, because you also wrestled with your Father's will before you went to the cross. Yet you ultimately completed your Father's will in every way. Help me to be still & deeply listen to your voice, and to keep surrendering to your Father's will as you did.

MY CITY

Let your will be done in my city as it is in heaven. It can be:
☐ overwhelming   ☐ tiring   ☐ numbing   ☐ hopeful
☐ ....

to contemplate all the city's problems where it seems like your good will, justice, and mercy are far from being done, like:
☐ poverty & hunger
☐ inequalities of all kinds
☐ sexual exploitation
☐ corporate corruption
☐ financial crises
☐ ....

Let your mercy & power come to do your will.

MY RESPONSE

From my own heart to the problems in the world, help me recognize our deep need for your will and restoration. Give me wisdom to know the specific needs in my city and of my "neighbours" where you want me to participate in bringing your

☐ mercy.   ☐ compassion.   ☐ hope. ☐ ....

Show me practical ways and give me opportunities to love my neighbours and city as Jesus would with compassion.
☐ ....
☐ ....

Thank you for your perfect will, Father God.

MY REFLECTIONS & ACTIONS

☐ New knowledge, revelations or thoughts about God that came (and what difference that makes to my journey):

☐ Heart changes I felt happen during prayer, or that I felt God wanting me to change in the coming days:

☐ Next steps (decisions, actions, etc.):

MY GRATITUDE

Thank you God for:

Thanks for hearing my prayers. Give me eyes to see how you will answer in your time & in your way. Empower me to participate in how you answer.

IN JESUS' NAME, AMEN

Our Daily Bread

Earthly riches are full of poverty.
Augustine

*I experienced today the most exquisite
pleasure I ever had in my life. I was able
to breathe freely for above five minutes.*
A Young Invalid

*Life cannot be satisfied when it is
lived out as a consuming entity.*
Ravi Zecharias

"Give us this day our daily bread" are simple words that summarize all our prayers for earthly concerns. "Bread" is more than food. It also refers to the Word of God. Jesus said, "Man does not live by bread alone but by every word that proceeds from the mouth of God." Bread refers to the enjoyment of the gospel and faith in God.

It is also a metaphor for all of life's necessities. When we ask for daily bread we ask for good government and good health. We also ask for good health, so that we can enjoy our food. Robbie Burns penned a prayer

Some ha' meat that canna' eat.
Some na' ha' meat that want it.
We ha' meat, and we ca' eat
Sa the Lord be thanked.

When we pray for daily bread, our request has a specific meaning as well as a comprehensive application. We are asking for all of life's necessities as well as the peace and health to enjoy them.

Asking for daily bread slowly changes our entire outlook on life

As we pray this amazing prayer we not only receive what we ask for – bread – we also discover that Jesus is transforming us. First, he is teaching us trust and thankfulness. Second, he is building generosity and kindness. Third, Jesus is developing our contentment and simplicity of life. We become what we pray.

1. As we pray, we learn trust and thankfulness

As we humbly ask, "Give us this day our daily bread," we acknowledge that all good things come from God. When we credit our own labor and industry for the prosperity we enjoy, we are denying that life is a gift.

In Canada, a wealthy person puts in a long day to make a good living. In Calcutta, a rickshaw driver works day and night to make a few rupees. If a person is poor, it often has nothing to do with how industrious he is. He or she may not have the opportunity to make a good living.

When we pray for bread, "we lift up empty hands." We depend on God to fill all our needs from his own bounty and kindness. Asking for daily bread involves turning from self-reliance and asking for a heart that relies on God.

Trust in God's provision is enriched with thankfulness of heart

The habit of asking implies a response of thanksgiving. There is no greater proof of Jesus' work in our hearts than genuine thankfulness. Thanksgiving is an antidote to greed and to envy. When we give thanks we take our eyes off what we do not have.

Just as the world looks smaller from the window of a plane at 35,000 feet, in thankful prayer we rise above daily problems and see the abundance of God. It is amazing how discontent with the bills, mortgage, and expenses of life disappears when we give thanks for the abundance on our table each day.

Achieving thankfulness is at the heart of Jesus' plan for his people. When the Israelites returned from the Babylonian captivity and rebuilt the city walls, their leaders "assigned two large choirs to give thanks."

To the believers at Philippi Paul explains how thankfulness cures worry:

Philippians 4:6,7

Do not be anxious about anything, but in everything, by prayer and petition, with thanksgiving, present your requests to God. And the peace of God, which transcends all understanding, will guard your hearts and your minds in Christ Jesus.

As we pray, we move from anxiety and restlessness about possessions to a spirit of "joyfully giving thanks." When we start our day, or begin a meal with simple thankfulness, we are cultivating an attitude of contentment and inner joy.

2. As we pray, we learn kindness and generosity

We do not ask "Give me this day my daily bread." We pray "give us this day our daily bread." This is a prayer for others as much as it is a prayer for ourselves. We also pray for our friends, neighbors, family – indeed, our country and whole world – to have daily bread. We love our neighbor in prayer. We are also to love our neighbor in deeds:

1John 4:20

If anyone has material possessions and sees his brother in need but has no pity on him, how can the love of God be in him? No one can say they love God, whom they cannot see, if they do not love their brother whom they do see.

Jesus' parable of the Good Samaritan teaches us never to discriminate when it comes to compassion and kindness. The wounded and naked person on the roadside is Jewish. While Jewish religious types walk by the other side of the road, the Samaritan – whose people were sworn enemies of the Jews – bandages and feeds his enemy. This foreigner's love for God is evidenced in his compassion.

Luke 10

When we pray this prayer we ask for a generous spirit

When we ask for daily bread, we ask for the ability and willingness to give an increasing portion of what we have to others in need. Jesus says, "Freely you have received. Freely give." No matter how much we make or own, we ask to be content with a modest portion. We pray for courage and integrity to give sacrificially to Christ's mission and to those in need.

Christian giving is sacrificial because it is modeled on the sacrifice of Jesus:

For you know the grace of our Lord Jesus Christ, that though he was rich, yet for your sakes he became poor, so that you through his poverty might become rich.

2 Corinthians 8:9

Jesus says "Love your neighbor as yourself." This means we should love and care for ourselves as well as for our neighbor. Life is meant to be lived in balance. Our life is a "mini Trinity" of relationships – God, others and self. A balanced person divides and balances his or her time, energy and resources on God first, others second and self third.

However, anything near this balance is rare. On average, each of us spends more than 95 per cent of life's income on ourselves. No matter how we slice it, this is not a life of balance. There is too little left for God and others.

This lack of balance leads to ill health and a poor state of mind. We can trace a good deal of spiritual unhappiness and discontent to a preoccupation with self. As we follow Jesus in day-by-day prayer for bread, God will lead us to a life of kindness and generosity – to a life of balance.

3. As we pray we learn contentment and simplicity

When we ask God for "this day's" bread, we are called to seek God's provision one day at a time. We leave tomorrow to him.

This is the lesson of the manna.

The children of Israel are led through a wilder-ness for forty years. God provides them daily bread – called manna. It contains everything they need in the way of nourishment. However, it only lasts that day. It rots overnight.

God provides his children a lesson of daily trust in this. He teaches the Israelites to look to him one day at a time to give them all they need. When we ask "this day" for bread, we ask for a portion of life's blessings that is enough for this day. We do not ask for too little – so that we could not pay our bills, provide for our dependents, and help those in need. Yet, we ask for bread, not a life of luxury and indulgence.

When we ask for daily bread, we leave it in God's hands to decide how much or how little is right for us. He can take us through times of want and scarcity. We may have savings accounts, insurance and retirement plans, but if we are not careful these "storehouses" become a substitute for daily reliance upon God!

Jesus tells us a simple and powerful parable about this "storehouse" problem:

"The ground of a certain rich man produced a good crop. He thought to himself, 'What shall I do? I have no place to store my crops.' "Then he said, 'This is what I'll do. I will tear down my barns and build bigger ones, and there I will store all my grain and my goods. And I'll say to myself, "You have plenty of good things laid up for many years. Take life easy; eat, drink and be merry." "But God said to him, 'You fool! This very night your life will be demanded from you. Then who will get what you have prepared for yourself?' "This is how it will be with anyone who stores up things for himself but is not rich toward God."

Luke 12:16-21

God knows what each of his children can handle. God knows what we need.

He knows how much we need. He has a perfect plan for us. Poverty or riches is not the issue – contentment is. Just look, he says, at the world he has created:

Therefore I tell you, do not worry about your life, what you will eat or drink; or about your body, what you will wear.... Look at the birds of the air; they do not sow or reap or store away in barns, and yet your heavenly Father feeds them. Are you not much more valuable than they? Who of you by worrying can add a single hour to his life? And why do you worry about clothes? See how the lilies of the field

Matthew 6:25-29,33-34

grow. They do not labor or spin. Yet I tell you that not even Solomon in all his splendor was dressed like one of these. But seek first his kingdom and his righteousness, and all these things will be given to you as well. Therefore do not worry about tomorrow, for tomorrow will worry about itself. Each day has enough trouble of its own.

Each time I pray this prayer for daily bread, I take time to thank God for the various kinds of "daily bread" I enjoy. I ask God to help me to trust him one day at a time. I ask him to forgive and still my restless need to store up for tomorrow.

Asking for "bread" encourages a life of simplicity

Bread is wonderful. Walk into any bakery early in the morning and you know what I mean. The aroma stirs every hungry cell. Yet bread is the simplest of foods.

In this petition we ask to live with increasing simplicity. Simplicity is difficult for us. When we sell a house at a good profit, inherit some money, or receive a raise or bonus, without thinking, we immediately plan how to spend or save it. We make our lives more cluttered than before! In our aptly named "consumer culture," this habit of increased acquisition seems obvious and right. In contrast, Jesus' call to simplicity seems quaint or absurd.

However, following Jesus and praying this prayer has radical consequences. Simplicity becomes a beautiful thing. Luxury and self-indulgence become ugly.

Prayerful Pondering

DAY   1   2   3   4   **5**   6   7

I   What are you thankful for today?

2   Where are you struggling with anxiety or self-reliance, concerning your daily practical needs? Where do you want to learn to trust God for tomorrow?

3   How much are your heart and life characterized by contentment? In what ways do you struggle with self-indulgence, desire for accumulating more, or greed?

4   How much of your time/talent/treasure are you storing and spending on yourself? How much are you sharing with others? With God?

5   How much of your prayer is thanksgiving? How much is asking for things?

Prayer Prompts

When we pray for "Our daily bread":

* We thank God for all that we have, recognizing it all as a grace from him. We ask for a spirit of thankfulness, contentment with what we have, simplicity in our living, and generosity with what he has given us.

* We ask God to provide for our earthly needs. We confess our anxieties and our self-sufficiency. We ask for a heart that trusts and relies on God.

* We rise above the anxiety of daily problems and see the abundance of God. We surrender our restless need to store up for tomorrow.

* We pray for a spirit of generosity and kindness, so that we have courage and integrity to give sacrificially to those in need and who are on God's heart.

* We pray for our country and world to have daily bread. We ask for good government, wisdom for public leaders and policy makers, peace and health to enjoy life's necessities.

Spend some time in thanksgiving and praise. Write your own gratitude list. Taking time at meal times is an easy place to start.

My Personal Prayers

DAY 1 2 3 4 **5** 6 7

TO: Father God   **TODAY IS:** MM/DD/YY

PRAYER SPOT @ ☐ WORK ☐ HOME ☐ SCHOOL ☐

PRIORITY: Trusting you for TODAY's NEEDS

REQUEST: Be our PROVIDER

MY LIFE

When I pause to think about it, you have been so generous to me. Thank you for the many kinds of "daily bread" you provide:

☐ a roof over my head

☐ food on the table

☐ good health to enjoy life

☐ abilities that enable me to work for a living

☐ meaningful relationships

☐

☐

Even with this abundance, I admit my focus can instead be on lusting after what I do not have because of:

☐ my desire for comfort & pleasure

☐ self-indulgence

☐ greed

☐ trying to save too far ahead because I like having security/control

☐

☐

I confess my prayers are often:
- ☐ asking you to meet my own selfish needs
- ☐ asking you only to solve my problems & remove my stresses
- ☐ ....
- ☐ ....

...rather than growing in trusting you more. You already know all my needs and how to best meet them.
- ☐ Help me to trust you to provide for my specific needs.
- ☐ Help me to recognize & thank you for your provision.
- ☐ Forgive my restless need to store up for tomorrow.
- ☐ ....
- ☐ ....

Thank you that you ultimately provided Jesus to be our Bread of life to meet our deepest needs.
- ☐ Teach me to be satisfied with you so that I'm not lusting after things that can't meet my heart hunger like only you can.
- ☐ Give me a growing uneasiness with the world's life-draining chase to accumulate & push for more. Grant me strength to challenge the consumer culture.
- ☐ Teach me daily reliance on you, gratitude, contentment & simplicity so that I can live generously.
- ☐ ....
- ☐ ....

MY CITY

I pray for you to meet the needs of my city. I pray for our city's decision makers and leaders in government, business, finance, education, science, arts, etc. Bless them to be peace makers, empowered by your wisdom to navigate challenging times and resolve complex conflicts. I pray for the peace and health of the city so that we can be generous in the global scene.

MY RESPONSE

Teach me to be a wise manager of all you've given me. What practical ways are you asking me to invest:

☐ my time & energy...

☐ my talents & abilities...

☐ my treasures & material wealth...

...to extend your grace & blessing to people in my life & city.

MY REFLECTIONS & ACTIONS

☐ New knowledge, revelations or thoughts about God that came (and what difference that makes to my journey):

☐ Heart changes I felt happen during prayer, or that I felt God wanting me to change in the coming days:

☐ Next steps (decisions, actions, etc.):

MY GRATITUDE

Thank you God for:

Thanks for hearing my prayers. Give me eyes to see how you will answer in your time & in your way. Empower me to participate in how you answer.

IN JESUS' NAME, AMEN

Forgive Us

OUR DEBTS AS WE FORGIVE OUR DEBTORS

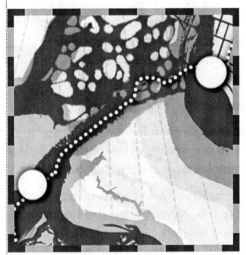

*Criticism of others nails them
to the past. Prayer for others
releases them to the future.*
Frank Laubach

*We cannot be wrong with man
and right with God.*
"The Kneeling Christian"

I t is curious that Jesus leaves this urgent necessity towards the end of his prayer. Why did he not start with forgiveness?

In his prayer, Jesus puts God first. He teaches us to do the same. Jesus also wants us to know how to approach God, so we know what to ask forgiveness for. "Our Father" sets the relational context which permits a humble, courageous approach to God – faults and all. If we do not come to God as father, we will tend to approach him as a forbidding judge.

What we need to be forgiven of

We need to be forgiven for our sins. But what is sin? There is no easy answer to this question. Seneca said, "Sin is complex and admits infinite variations."

Sin concerns wrong behavior. You know the list – idolatry, murder, promiscuity, stealing and lying. Yet we know sin goes deeper. It includes our thoughts and motives: hatred, envy, greed, malice, pride, and self-righteousness. Jesus said, "Whoever nurses anger against a brother has committed murder."

Sin is more than isolated actions or thoughts. All sin is deeply personal and relational. When we sin we offend God, others, and self. Think about it. If we choose another god to worship besides God Almighty, we "cheat" on him. Similarly, when we steal from someone, we undermine our bond with them.

Sin is serious. It wounds people and breaks relationships. The only way to restore these relationships is for Jesus to be wounded and broken for us.

The high price for our forgiveness

After viewing Mel Gibson's *The Passion of the Christ,*
many wondered why Jesus had to suffer so brutally.
Hours of whipping, a wreath of thorns, spitting and
mocking, hands being nailed to rough sawn wood,
all drawn out in painful, graphic detail.

Is this overkill?

The answer is "No!" Forgiveness is free but it is not
cheap. The highest price possible is paid that we might
receive forgiveness as a free gift. The brutality of the
cross is a measure of the horror of human sin.
Put all hatred, malice, envy, lust, deceit, betrayal –
and all the wars, rapes, genocides, abuse and oppression
in humankind's sad history and you will understand
the infinite price required and paid to remove our sin
and provide forgiveness forever.

Yet, Jesus' death is not a tragedy. His suffering
conquers sin and defeats death at the cross. It achieves
reconciliation for you when you come to God for
forgiveness of any crime, cruelty, or injustice. All you
have to do is humbly ask.

When you confess your sins you are completely washed
clean of them. An old saying captures this truth:

That Jesus died on the cross is history.
That Jesus died for sin is theology.
That Jesus died for my sin is Christianity.

As you read this, remember why Jesus died. Ask him
to apply his sacrifice to you and to forgive your sins.
Become the renewed person he died for you to be.

The challenge of receiving forgiveness

The prick of our conscience often makes us aware of the seriousness of sin. But we need great assurances from God in order to find the humility and courage to confess our sins. We need the promises of God:

Isaiah 1:18

Though your sins are like scarlet, they shall be as white as snow; though they are red as crimson, they shall be like wool.

1 John 1:9

If we confess our sins, he is faithful and just and will forgive us our sins and purify us from all unrighteousness.

It takes grace to confess, and grace to receive forgiveness. We struggle with residual guilt, rehearsing our faults again and again. What can we do about our reluctance to receive forgiveness? We must remember these great promises in Scripture. And we must remind ourselves that God forgets our sin once he forgives it.

Forgiveness is as complete and finished as the perfect sacrifice of Jesus

This verse tells how Jesus is the only one who can remove the guilt and the power of sin:

1 John 2:1-2

If anybody does sin, we have one who speaks to the Father in our defense—Jesus Christ, the Righteous One. He is the atoning sacrifice for our sins and not only for ours but also for the sins of the whole world.

The principle is this – don't dwell on your sin and guilt, but look steadily at Jesus. His sacrifice has infinite value to cancel your debt. Your sins are forever nailed to the cross.

The challenge and joy of learning to forgive others

When we ask for forgiveness it is "as we forgive our debtors." Receiving forgiveness is only half the picture. Jesus teaches that we are to extend forgiveness to others, as well, without exception:

For if you forgive men when they sin against you, your heavenly Father will also forgive you but if you do not forgive men their sins, your Father will not forgive your sins.

Matthew 6:14

Jesus tells us to forgive without excuse for how often or how deep the offense:

When Peter came to Jesus and asked, "Lord, how many times shall I forgive my brother when he sins against me? Up to seven times?" Jesus answered, "I tell you, not seven times, but seventy-seven times."

Matthew 18:21

Overlooking a fault is possible in the "misdemeanors" of life. A rough word, minor neglect, or criticism – such wounds often heal in their own time.

What are we to do, however, with the "felonies" of life? Consider victims of adultery and wrongful divorce. Or those who are defrauded in business and investments and lose everything. Who can heal their bitter disappointment? Forgiveness and reconciliation can seem like a distant dream.

Yet, the victim can never be fully healed without forgiveness. The torn relationship will continue to bring pain. A bitter and unforgiving heart will only hurt the victim.

Jesus understands the danger of not forgiving others. There are at least three very good reasons for Jesus' strong stand on forgiving others. *First, by reason of comparison.* The debt owed to us cannot compare with the debt we owe to God. Nor can the small sacrifice I pay to forgive someone compare with the price Jesus paid.

The second reason is logic. When we ask for forgiveness we need to confess all of our sins. Over years Miroslav Volf struggled with hatred and a desire for revenge against the Serbian forces that ravaged his Croatian homeland. God taught him the important lesson about forgiving others:

We must not forget that there is an evil worse than the original crime. It consists of self-centered slothfulness of the mind, heart, and will that will not recognize one's own sinfulness, not pursue justice for the innocent, and not extend grace to the guilty.
Miroslav Volf

A third reason we forgive others is that not forgiving can kill our heart. "Unforgiveness is the poison I drink trying to kill you." An unforgiving heart breeds grudges and bitterness – eventually killing the capacity to love. When we harbor an unforgiving heart, we rob ourselves of the release of forgiveness.

Sin is a kind of toxic waste that lasts forever if not removed by forgiveness. There was a company that tried to drill a mile-deep hole to bury toxic waste. A few years later poisonous water surfaced. PCBs contaminated the water, which seeped upwards through cracks and crevices in the underground rock.

This is how sin works.

The only hope is concerted prayer as we ask for a spirit of contrition and confession – and wait for God to cleanse the soil and water of our sin.

God gives power and hope to forgive others

For those wounded without an apology there is hope. Jesus not only died to forgive us of our sins. He gave his life to heal us of every wound we have had to suffer in a sinful and violent world:

Surely he took up our infirmities and carried our sorrows, the punishment that brought us peace was upon him, and by his wounds we are healed.

Isaiah 53:5

This healing makes it possible for us to forgive others – from the heart. Even while you are healing, you can also take your "enemy" to Jesus in prayer. Prayer is the first and most important step in restoring relations with others:

I can no longer condemn or hate a brother for whom I pray, no matter how much trouble he causes me.
Dietrich Bonhoeffer

Then, when your heart is ready and it is safe to do so, Jesus encourages you to go to your offender to seek reconciliation, in order to help them acknowledge their sin and move towards reconciliation.

If your brother sins against you, go and show him his fault, just between the two of you. If he listens to you, you have won your brother over.

Matthew 18:15

This "intervention" requires wisdom and patience. We must ask for love and courage in order to be effective. We must also ask for God to open the door for the right opportunity. As he hears our prayers the hope for reconciliation becomes real.

In my own life, it took years of prayer for me to gather the courage to speak to someone who had hurt me. Fear of rejection kept me from seeing the truth – or even acknowledging my hurt and their fault. I prayed about this. Then one day we got together and God opened the door for meaningful conversation.

It went wonderfully. In fact, after willingly acknowledging his fault, this person also confronted me about my resentment and arrogance. We both felt better afterwards. We experienced reconciliation through forgiveness. Our relationship has been growing ever since.

Forgiveness results in relational reconciliation

Reconciliation is the key to lasting and growing relationships with others. I think of my marriage. Caron and I have been together for over thirty years, and through many bumps and bruises our love has continually grown. The key is not compatibility or strength of character. The secret is reconciliation through forgiveness.

Saying "Sorry" and "I forgive you" improves a marriage. Parent-child relationships also grow and deepen with an honest admission of failings – on both sides.

In the workplace and public arena we experience power politics, labor strife, racial and class conflict. Without reconciliation we will destroy each other. Jesus says, "Blessed are the peacemakers." A Christian peacemaker is someone who prays and works for reconciliation because he has been forgiven and reconciled to God. God promises answers to our prayer:

Seek the peace and prosperity of the city to which I have carried you into exile. Pray to the Lord for it, because if it prospers, you too will prosper.

Jeremiah 29:7

The practice of forgiveness can be applied to every relationship – no matter how deep the problem. Broken family relationships need healing. Marriages lie in scattered shards of unresolved hurt. Friends are separated by careless words. An office team loses friendship and chemistry. A church is reduced to gossip and accusation. Fill in your own blank. Nothing is beyond the reach of Jesus.

Prayerful Pondering

DAY 1 2 3 4 5 6 7

I   How do you view the concept of "sin"? In light of God's holiness and glory as the standard, what areas of your life – thoughts, motives, words, actions – might God be bringing to light for you to confess? Ask him to show you your "filthy rags" as well as your "righteous riches."

2   How has your sin – thoughts, motives, words, actions – affected you, the people around you, and your relationship with God?

3   Where do you struggle to confess an area of sin to receive forgiveness – either something you feel unworthy of, (a sin that feels to too difficult to forgive), or something you feel unapologetic for (a sin that you don't see as a sin)?

4   Where do you struggle with an unforgiving heart? How has holding onto unforgiveness affected your life? Are you able to bring it to Jesus as a first step?

5   Which situational or relational conflicts in the immediate world around you could use your prayers and peacemaking actions?

Sin is an archery term that simply means to "miss the mark." Often we think of sin simply as the obvious external negative deeds we commit, such lying, cheating, or stealing.

Yet we must also be mindful to equally confess our "righteous deeds" – the things that we rely on to justify our own righteousness and goodness to stand before God. Compared to God's holiness, even our righteous deeds are filthy rags.

Taking it deeper, God also reveals our sin at a deeper level – to our thoughts, attitudes and motives. Even doing an externally good act with a bad attitude or for an ill motive is sin that should be confessed at the cross.

Prayer Prompts

When we pray "Forgive us our sins as we forgive those who have sinned against us":

* We thank Jesus for the high price he paid to make forgiveness and reconciliation possible. We bring our hearts to Jesus, asking for courage and humility to acknowledge and confess our sin.

* We receive God's cleansing of our sin through Jesus' sacrifice and joyfully accept God's free and abundant grace. We bring our wounds to Jesus and his healing streams.

* As we are forgiven, and as we are healing, we find grace, courage, and power to forgive others who have sinned against us. We bring them to Jesus in prayer. We ask for God to open the door for the right opportunities for reconciliation.

* We pray to be peacemakers in the relationships and situations in the world around us.

My Personal Prayers

TO: Father God   **TODAY IS:** MM/DD/YY

PRAYER SPOT @ ☐ WORK   ☐ HOME   ☐ SCHOOL ☐

PRIORITY: Receiving FORGIVENESS & seeking RECONCILED RELATIONSHIPS

REQUEST: FORGIVE & cancel our debts God as we forgive others

MY LIFE

Thank you that you are a forgiving God. Thank you for the confidence we have to approach you because of Jesus, knowing that you are faithful and just to forgive us when we confess our sin.

I admit that my reaction to confession and sin is:

☐ to be too proud to admit or see it

☐ not feel I've done anything wrong

☐ avoid it

☐ focus so much on it and feel immense guilt

☐

☐

Give me humility and courage to confess and agree with you about my sin as you see it, in light of your perfect holiness. What are the things I have done that are wrong in your sight

☐ in my actions & habits...

☐ in my thoughts...

☐ in my attitudes...

What are the "righteous deeds" that I rely on to make myself acceptable in your eyes, areas where I feel I deserve all credit and glory?

☐ in my actions...

☐ in my thoughts...

☐ in my attitudes...

Is there anyone whom I need to ask forgiveness from:
☐ who I have hurt
☐ who I've held a grudge against
☐ who I've been impatient with
☐

I'm sorry for what I've done. Forgive me of my sin and guilt. Thank you Jesus for living your sinless life on earth as a sacrifice to make forgiveness possible, and restoring my relationship with God. Thank you for cleansing me as white as snow.

MY LIFE

As I receive your amazing grace and forgiveness, empower me to be gracious to forgive others as you forgive me. I want to talk with you about:

☐ a specific offense that has caused me to feel hurt

☐ a difficult relationship that is causing me grief

☐ a person that has hurt me in the past that I can't seem to let go of and keeps affecting me today

☐

Give me the heart to be willing to forgive. I admit I am struggling because I feel towards them:

☐ resentment

☐ anger

☐ bitterness

☐

☐

Forgive me for these feelings. Jesus, give me the strength you had when you endured the ultimate injustices against you when you were betrayed, mocked and killed without just cause. Fill me with your love, mercy, willingness and courage to forgive.

I choose to forgive the things they did, and the things they didn't do, that hurt me. Specifically, I forgive them for:

- [ ] betraying me
- [ ] not being there for me, neglecting me or abandoning me
- [ ] rejecting me, or not accepting me for who I am
- [ ] nagging me & rarely saying anything positive to me
- [ ]
- [ ]

Jesus, help me to forgive where it's difficult. You gave the command to forgive, so please help me to do it. I forgive them with all my heart.

Father God, I place them in your hands. I know you will treat them according to your justice (and not my own sense of justice as you don't need my help). I know you will also treat them with your mercy, the same way you treat me with mercy. I set them free. I drop any desire for vengeance. I set myself free from what this has cost me:

- [ ] money
- [ ] energy expended worrying, including lost nights of sleep
- [ ] a broken relationship
- [ ]
- [ ]

PRIORITY: Receiving FORGIVENESS & seeking RECONCILED RELATIONSHIPS

REQUEST: FORGIVE & cancel our debts God as we forgive others

MY LIFE

Knowing all this has cost me, I cancel their debts to me.
They owe me nothing. They don't owe me an apology. They
don't have to change their behaviour. They don't owe me
anything, and I don't owe them anything, except to love
them, as the Bible tells me. As I have forgiven them for
everything. God please:

☐ heal my heart

☐ take away the pain & hurt

☐ tell me your truth about the situation

☐

☐

Help me to supernaturally keep forgiving, every time this
comes up in my heart and life until it is completely clear.

MY CITY

When I look at my city, I pray for the areas and issues that
need reconciliation and healing:

☐ families & households to grow in resolving hurt & conflict

☐ personal & business relationships to grow beyond conflict

☐ political cooperation

☐ racial reconciliation

☐ unity of your church

☐

☐

I pray for you to preserve the peace of the city. Work in these
difficult places. Empower individuals with your love & forgivness.
Help me to be a peacemaker in my interactions & relationships.

MY REFLECTIONS & ACTIONS

☐ New knowledge, revelations or thoughts about God that came (and what difference that makes to my journey):

☐ Heart changes I felt happen during prayer, or that I felt God wanting me to change in the coming days:

☐ Next steps (decisions, actions, etc.):

MY GRATITUDE

Thank you God for:

Thanks for hearing my prayers. Give me eyes to see how you will answer in your time & in your way. Empower me to participate in how you answer.

IN JESUS' NAME, AMEN

Lead Us

NOT INTO TEMPTATION
BUT DELIVER US FROM EVIL

To have prayed well is to have fought well.

Edward McKendree Bounds

The devil trembles when he sees God's weakest child on his knees.

Anonymous

P*ilgrim's Progress* by John Bunyan is one of the most popular parables in the English language. The main character, Christian, is on a pilgrimage from the City of Destruction to the Celestial City.

He faces seen and unseen foes. He falls into the Slough of Despond, spends time in Doubting Castle and is tempted by sensual pleasure and ambition in the city Vanity Fair. In a crucial battle, he goes head to head with Apollyon, (another name for Satan) who is the malevolent "ruler of this world." Christian defends himself with the shield of faith and the sword of truth. He is guarded by "All Prayer" – the comprehensive defense and weapon of faith.

Bunyan's imagery is close to the Biblical language and metaphor. The Christian life is a war within a journey. We need prayer for the battle. We need prayer for the journey – each and every day. When we pray, "Lead us not into temptation, but deliver us from evil," we are asking for at least four things. First, we ask for God to lead us. Second, we pray for eyes of faith. Third, we ask God to defend us from temptations and trials. Fourth, we ask for God's guiding presence & power.

1. In this journey we ask for God to lead us

When we pray "lead us not into temptation," we are implicitly asking our heavenly father to be our guide and companion through the journey and battles of life until, safe at last, we come home to his heavenly kingdom.

God taught the lesson of his leading to the Israelites as they journeyed for forty years through the wilderness. He went before them in a pillar of cloud by day and a pillar of fire by night. The pillar is a picture of the Holy Spirit. Being led by that Spirit is a summary of the Christian journey:

Those who are led by the Spirit of God are sons of God.

Romans 8:14

When we pray "lead us not into temptation," we acknowledge that life's path is often hard and painful. "Temptation" is used in its original sense, to mean trial and testing. When we ask God to lead us, we are praying that he will give us grace to face, courage to endure, and power to overcome that kind of temptation.

Jesus provides the perfect example of following his heavenly father when he faces trial and testing in the Garden of Gethsemane:

Going a little farther, he fell with his face to the ground and prayed, "My Father, if it is possible, may this cup be taken from me. Yet not as I will, but as you will."

Matthew 26:39

Jesus is asking, if possible, to be led away from the last temptation – dying on a cross. At the same time he is praying for grace to accept God's leading and for courage to endure it.

We share our prayer with Jesus when we pray "Lead us not into temptation." We experience suffering and loss. We endure. Following him, we come through to victory.

2. To advance, we need to see the whole picture

Albert Einstein was perhaps the greatest genius of the twentieth century. When he devised the theories of special and general relativity, it was assumed that he discovered the key to understanding the universe.

However, as late as 1924 Einstein and everyone else thought that the Milky Way constituted the universe. Now we know that there are as many as 100 billion other galaxies in the universe – each with more than 100 billion stars! Einstein "saw" only a small part of the picture.

In much the same way, the world before our eyes is only a small part of life. We should invite new discovery, welcome new paradigms and not hold tightly to a safe and familiar picture. We can continue to explore and enjoy the universe we see, but be open to a far greater reality of which this seen world is only a part.

Where does prayer fit in this? Prayer is like a spiritual Hubble telescope, lifting us far above the earth's perspective to see the entire cosmos like God sees it. As we pray, glimpses of invisible galaxies come into view.

This directly relates to our request, "Lead us not into temptation." Because God creates everything visible and invisible, these two "halves" of existence are deeply related and in constant interplay. Forces of good and evil are in constant conflict.

This is the Christian worldview. Every person, community, church, and Christian is engaged in a very real battle against temptation, guilt, and despair. The instrument of attack can be other people, social forces, media, unseen personalities, or simply one's own unbelief and self-doubt.

This fight matters. If we quit and give in there will be no victory. Yet ultimately, in the final hour, Jesus himself will physically appear with his angels and defeat all of his and our enemies.

Be self-controlled and alert. Your enemy the devil prowls around like a roaring lion looking for someone to devour. Resist him, standing firm in the faith, because you know that your brothers throughout the world are undergoing the same kind of sufferings. And the God of all grace, who called you to his eternal glory in Christ, after you have suffered a little while, will himself restore you and make you strong, firm and steadfast. To him be the power for ever and ever. Amen.

1 Peter 5:8-11

Prayer connects us to the power and presence of Jesus, our coming King. As we pray in expectation, his resurrection life flows into our hearts by the Holy Spirit he gives us. He enables us to defend against every seen and unseen enemy, and to advance in his promised victory.

3. We pray to overcome temptation

In this visible/invisible battle we fight different varieties of temptation on different fronts. There are at least four battle lines where temptation occurs.

First, we are tempted through the weakness of our fallen nature. Inordinate desire, deviant passion, envy and avarice, arrogance, hatred, and pride are within each of us. This "interior dislocation of the soul" (Dorothy Sayers) accounts for much of the bloodshed, brokenness, and betrayal found in the human story. Our own inner compulsion (not God or the devil) leads us into every temptation:

When tempted, no one should say, "God is tempting me." For God cannot be tempted by evil, nor does he tempt anyone; but each one is tempted when, by his own evil desire, he is dragged away and enticed. Then, after desire has conceived, it gives birth to sin; and sin, when it is full grown, gives birth to death.

James 1:13-15

Second, temptation surrounds us. As pollution clogs the air of the cities of the world, so we live in an atmosphere of temptation. We need prayer to breathe the fresh air of heaven. And we need it in special measure in a world where media has made the lure of temptation far more potent. For example, sexual exploitation and predation are fueled by "sexy" magazine covers, promiscuous sitcoms, salacious talk shows, and seductive advertising. Through the Internet, base passions are excited in increasing frequency and intensity.

Little is being done to slow the avalanche. We reserve moral outrage for those who would try to restrict our access to this "information." One person noted, "Even to avoid evil makes one a marked man." We pray fervently to withstand temptation because we are constantly surrounded by it.

Third, moral and spiritual assault comes in the form of false teaching. Take the popular adventure novel *The Da Vince Code,* which represents Jesus as a pagan leader who participated in ritual sex and sired children through Mary Magdalene. Though none of the alleged documents the author uses to support his argument have ever been discovered, he represents this lie as history.

Because so few know the Bible's portrait of Jesus, enormous numbers are drawn in and are dead serious about his viewpoints. (*Breaking the Da Vinci Code* by Peter Jones is a good antidote.) The Bible warns that in every age, new "Christs" will arise. The objective of these "antichrists" is to mislead believers and to prevent others from getting to know who Jesus really is:

Matthew 24:4,5

Jesus answered: "Watch out that no one deceives you.
For many will come in my name, claiming, 'I am the Christ,'
and will deceive many."

When we pray, "Lead us not into temptation" we pray
for faith to resist false teachings about Christ.

Fourth, the trials, sufferings and betrayals of life tempt us
to question or even abandon our faith in God. It is really
this doubting of God which is at the root of
every temptation.

Our spiritual life is like a ship. Faith is the hull. In naval
warfare, if the hull is strong and holds, little significant
damage results from a cannon attack. Only if cannon
balls pierce the hull is there penetration to the heart of
the vessel.

In the same way, every assault of evil is first directed
at this hull – our faith. Using accusation, trial, and
temptation, Satan wants to wreck our connection to
God and for us to question his goodness, power, and
love. If he succeeds – the hull is breached and we begin
to sink. Once we doubt the goodness, grace and power
of God we are immediately vulnerable.

On our own we are outgunned and outmanned by a
superior enemy. But as we pray, Jesus strengthens and
comforts us in temptation: "I have prayed that your faith
might stand." The apostle Paul encourages us:

1 Corinthians 10:13

God will not permit you to be tempted beyond what you are
able to endure but when you are tempted he will also provide
a way out that you may be able to withstand it.

Paul is not saying that we will never fall into sin.

What he means is that though we will be tempted and sometimes fail, by his grace and power we will grow in faith and live to fight another day.

As we ask God not to lead us into temptation our greatest encouragement is Jesus himself. He endured every temptation Satan could throw at him (Luke 4:1-13). One reason he did all this is so that he would be able to defend and protect us against every temptation we face:

Because he himself suffered when he was tempted, he is able to help those who are being tempted.

4. God's presence and power: how God's kingdom advances

This prayer moves from defense, "Lead us not into temptation" to advance, "Deliver us from evil." Ultimately we not only survive the battles of life, we win. The reason for this is Jesus. His victory over sin and death at the cross and empty tomb is decisive and complete. The present age is a brief moment of history and the final "wrap up" is soon coming.

It is like the end of World War II. The decisive battle for the Allied victory is fought at Normandy. After this battle it is only one year before complete surrender and the signing of treaties.

In prayer, by faith, a believer appropriates and participates in Jesus' victory in every spiritual and practical area of this life. The victory we share with Jesus is seen and unseen, practical and spiritual.

For example, we work with a local ministry for sexually exploited women and their children called Genesis Vancouver. When we pray for a sexually exploited woman to be delivered, we desire her to experience the grace of forgiveness and spiritual healing. We also ask for her to be delivered from the pimps, johns and abusive people who prey on her and use her as a slave. Anything less would be less than Jesus intends:

This is part of the prayer for the Kingdom: it is the prayer that the forces of destruction, of dehumanization, of anti-creation, of anti-redemption may be bound and gagged, and that God's good world may escape from being sucked down into their morass.

NT Wright

As John Wesley said, "There is no Christianity that is not a social Christianity." When we pray "Deliver us from evil" we include social justice and mercy:

What does the Lord require of you, O man, but to do justice, and to love mercy and to walk humbly with your God?

Micah 6:8

Prayer is the key to victory in all spiritual warfare. Karl Barth writes "When God's people clasp their hands in prayer, it is the beginning of an uprising against the disorder of the world."

When we pray, God will give us courage for each day's battle – and also promises to act:

For he will deliver the needy who cry out, the afflicted who have no one to help. He will take pity on the weak and the needy and save the needy from death. He will rescue them from oppression and violence, for precious is their blood in his sight.

Psalm 72:12-14

Prayerful Pondering

I   What battles are you personally fighting –
a habitual sin or temptation, a negative thought
pattern, cultural pressures, despair through a trial?
Consider that Jesus is praying for you. How does
this give you hope?

2   How can prayer give you courage?

3   Where do you need eyes of faith to see
God's perspective?

4   Where in the world around you do you see
conflict between light and dark forces?
What injustices can you pray for?

Prayer Prompts

When we pray "Lead us not into temptation, but deliver us from evil":

* We pray for eyes of faith to see from God's perspective the trials in our own lives, and to see the realities of spiritual forces in conflict in the world around us.

* We recognize God's guidance and presence with us, and Christ's resurrection power, to resist temptation, and to endure and overcome trials.

* We ask God to defend us with spiritual protection, and advance us in his power.

* We pray for others who are entangled in difficulties or trials, and pray for Jesus to defend and deliver them.

* We pray for the restraint of evil forces in our city and world. We pray for God's goodness and power to prevail.

My Personal Prayers

DAY   1   2   3   4   5   6   7

TO: Father God   **TODAY IS:** MM/DD/YY

PRAYER SPOT @ ☐ WORK ☐ HOME ☐ SCHOOL ☐

PRIORITY: Following God's LEADERSHIP & deliverance
REQUEST: RESCUE us God!

MY LIFE

You are a faithful and wise guide and companion who leads me through this journey of life.

You are always present, but I admit my spiritual sight can be weak to recognize you. I admit I often live more for the physical realm, not paying attention to the spiritual realm. My attention is diverted and my connection with you is interrupted by:

☐ distractions

☐ procrastination

☐ busyness

☐ laziness

☐ fear

☐ pride that says I don't need you

☐ suffering that tempts me to doubt your goodness

In my present trials and temptations, I feel:

☐ weak.   ☐ frustrated.   ☐ tired   ☐ stuck.   ☐ indifferent

☐ hopeful. ☐ willing to fight

☐

☐

☐

I want to overcome my temptations, but my inner compulsions threaten to overcome me. In my trials:

☐ Call my attention to your guidance, presence and power
☐ Fill me with grace and courage to endure.
☐ Give me eyes of faith to believe your power to deliver me.
☐
☐

Teach me your Word, your promises, the truth about who you really are. You are stronger than anything I face. Protect and defend me. Lead me forward where I most need.

MY CITY

Thank you Jesus that you knew temptation. At the beginning of your public ministry on earth you overcame the devil's temptations. As you prepared to leave this earth, you overcame the temptation to avoid your Father's difficult will for you to go to the cross. Thank you Jesus for praying for me and going before me. Deliver me from my battles so that I can also participate in the fight between good and evil in my city.

I pray for those who daily battle:

☐ addictions

☐ physical suffering or abuse

☐ mental health struggles

☐ unfair social structures & exploitation

Rescue and bring them near to you to know your compassion, presence and power in their challenges. I pray against the injustices and evils of:

☐ sexual exploitation

☐ corporate corruption

☐ oppression of the poor

☐ damage of the environment and your creation

☐

☐

Let your light shine stronger than the darkness. Show me the practical ways I can be involved in fighting the good fight in my city. Give me grace and courage to obey and walk in the light with you, leading me.

TO: Self

SUBJECT: My response to prayers about God's LEADERSHIP

MY REFLECTIONS & ACTIONS

☐ New knowledge, revelations or thoughts about God that came (and what difference that makes to my journey):

☐ Heart changes I felt happen during prayer, or that I felt God wanting me to change in the coming days:

☐ Next steps (decisions, actions, etc.):

MY GRATITUDE

Thank you God for:

Thanks for hearing my prayers. Give me eyes to see how you will answer in your time & in your way. Empower me to participate in how you answer. Thank you Jesus for praying for us individually by name, and for leading us.

IN JESUS' NAME, AMEN

AMEN
THE REST OF YOUR JOURNEY

*To be a Christian without prayer
is no more possible than to be
alive without breathing.*

Martin Luther

Our father in heaven
Hallowed be your name
Your kingdom come
Your will be done on earth as it is in heaven
Give us this day our daily bread
Forgive us our debts as we forgive our debtors
Lead us not into temptation
but deliver us from evil.

This is the prayer of Jesus, God's only Son. He always hears his Son. He will always hear the prayers of each of us, his adopted sons and daughters, as we pray it too. By giving us this prayer, Jesus is calling us to pray it faithfully. He invites us to pray it personally. He calls us to pray it as a community.

We find a dramatic illustration of the power of this call to pray in the *The Lord of the Rings* trilogy. In this Tolkien tale – and the movie series based on it – the citizens of Middle Earth have created a system of beacons, or signal fires. They are massive piles of dry timber, stacked in readiness on highly visible mountain tops. A lit torch is always ready. A pair of sentries will light the beacon the instant they are called.

This signal fire kindles the memory of ancient allegiances – a united people against a common enemy. When under attack, the ancient city of Gondor will light its beacons, and all of Middle Earth will gather to defend her. It is a summons and signal for the return of the King.

As the story unfolds, the great city of Gondor finds itself in trouble. Completely outnumbered, it is surrounded by legions of enemies. Huge catapults hurl monstrous rocks at it. A massive cast-iron battering ram tears through its gates. Behind this army is the hideous strength of Sauron – the evil spirit. His consuming purpose is to destroy the race of men and to prevent the return of the King.

Within the city is another enemy. Denethor, the steward of Gondor is assigned to protect the city and prepare for the coming king. He refuses to do his part. He has studied the might and power of his enemy and his heart is filled with despair. "All hope is lost," he says.

Worst of all, he refuses to light the beacons – to summon Middle Earth to war.

We see parallels in our present situation. We might value and enjoy our modern world, but our cities and our churches have enemies – without and within.

Relativism and hedonism break down the concept of truth and eat away at the foundations of right and wrong. There is no end of opponents attacking the simple truths of the gospel. "New Age," a return to the spirits of paganism, is growing. Television, radio, magazines, and the Internet bury us in advertising, shape us into voracious consumers and divert us from higher purposes. Relationships are reduced to sexual encounters.

This avalanche seems unstoppable. Ethical and religious concerns are dismissed and ridiculed. Many have resigned the field in frustration or despair. Some have joined the other side.

Behind this assault is an insidious, malevolent force. He is intent on crushing and eliminating any sense of eternal or transcendent purpose. In the meantime, within the city and within the church, like Denethor, the children of the King are strangely inactive. A foreboding calm settles over church and city. There is fear in the air. Our enemy smells it.

Yet there is a faithful remnant who knows what needs to be done. Jesus is calling us to light the beacons of prayer. When we pray Jesus' prayer we make a great discovery. We recover our identity as children of the king. At its heart, this prayer is a yearning for the return of the King to rescue and deliver all those who wait for him.

The difference prayer makes

In the battle for Middle Earth, the tide turns when the Gondor's beacon is lit. Seeing its flames, one beacon after another explodes in fire. The land is lit with hope. The long awaited king, Aragorn, sees the flaming beacons and prepares his return. It is time for him to assert his rightful rule and reign over Middle Earth. It is time to rescue the innocent. It is time to vanquish the enemy.

A similar scenario occurs when God's people set themselves to pray. To pray is to light the beacons. To pray Jesus' prayer is to summon the people of God to a united warfare of love and truth. It is a mighty cry for our king to lead us in battle.

Like flaming beacons, the fire of prayer is contagious. As this prayer begins to burn, the hearts of others will burn too. We unite to defend each other and to defend our neighbor and our cities. Hope replaces despair.

Readiness to act replaces apathy. We experience the might of grace to overcome hatred and violence.

The present and coming king himself will visit us.

At the critical moment, Aragorn the rightful king, returns to the city. The armies of Sauron have no defense against such an opponent. In a matter of minutes the city is regained, the besieged are rescued, and every foe is leveled to the ground.

Jesus is the present and coming king. When he comes, no enemy can withstand him. He storms the gates of the city in answer to prayer. He renews his church, transforms communities, rebuilds cities, and makes our streets safe to dwell in.

The seven purposes of Jesus will come to light as we pray his prayer. He gives us hearts that cry out "Abba. Father!" His kingdom will come. Men, women and children will be saved. His will shall be done in the streets of the city – with wisdom, love and courage. Simplicity and generosity will characterize his children. They will enjoy daily bread with thanksgiving. Bitter feuds will be resolved as we learn to receive and extend forgiveness. We will move from defending against temptations to advancing in spiritual battles.

He will hear and answer as we pray:

If my people who are called by my name, will humble themselves and pray – I will turn and heal their land.

Come Jesus Come!

Prayerful Pondering

I How have you seen God work through prayer during the course of reading this book?

2 How will you light your beacon?

3 Imagine: how would your life look if you began to consistently pray through the priorities of the Lord's prayer?

4 What are one or two ways you can integrate the Lord's prayer into your life?

My Personal Prayers

TO: Father God   **TODAY IS:** MM/DD/YY

PRAYER SPOT @ ☐ WORK ☐ HOME ☐ SCHOOL ☐

MY PRAYER

Dear God,
Here I am a little further in this journey of prayer...

Thank you for the good work you've started in my life through prayer. Continue the good work; keep teaching me how to pray. Here I am, ready to continue this adventure in prayer with you.

MY REFLECTIONS & ACTIONS

☐ New knowledge, revelations or thoughts about God that came (and what difference that makes to my journey):

☐ Heart changes I felt happen during prayer, or that I felt God wanting me to change in the coming days:

☐ Next steps (decisions, actions, etc.):

MY GRATITUDE

Thank you God for:

Thanks for hearing my prayers. Give me eyes to see how you will answer in your time & in your way. Empower me to participate in how you answer. Jesus, keep guiding me as I continue on in this journey of prayer.

IN JESUS' NAME, AMEN

My Personal Prayers

DAY 1   2   3   4   5   6   7   ∞

TO: Father God   **TODAY IS:** MM/DD/YY

PRAYER SPOT @ ☐ WORK ☐ HOME ☐ SCHOOL ☐

PRIORITY:

REQUEST:

MY LIFE

MY CITY

MY REFLECTIONS & ACTIONS

MY GRATITUDE

IN JESUS' NAME, AMEN

PUBLISHED BY

Prayer Current
Navigating Life Through Prayer

Prayer Current helps people navigate life
through prayer. Whether someone is just
entering the waters or is an experienced
traveler, Prayer Current provides
inspiration and practical tools
to grow in prayer, and to "pray it forward"
by helping grow others in prayer.

Designed for life in the city and for
personal or church use, Prayer Current
resources engage people in a balance
of reflection, interaction, study, actual
prayer practice and mission.

www.prayercurrent.com